EXECUTIVE
PRESENTATIONS
DEVELOP PRESENCE TO SPEAK
WITH CONFIDENCE AND SKILL

By
Jacqui Harper

Practical Inspiration
PUBLISHING

First published in Great Britain by Practical Inspiration Publishing, 2018

© Jacqui Harper, 2018
Cover design by Christian Bailey

The moral rights of the author have been asserted

ISBN 978-1-78860-016-3

ENDORSEMENTS

This book exudes Jacqui's trademark optimism, warmth and directness. She has unique credibility to write such a book because she has experience in the tough world of television news, she is a coach and an accomplished teacher. The book is full of sensible immensely practical advice on how to make presentations with impact. I am an experienced presenter myself but I learnt a lot from it, for instance the importance of how you actually walk on to that stage and how to use pauses. Whether you have to make short, powerful contributions in meetings or address 500 people in a conference centre, I strongly recommend this book for its distilled common sense and expert advice.

Jenny Rogers,
executive coach and author

This book should be required reading for anyone who needs to communicate via speeches!

Jacqui has produced a very useful and eminently practical book, covering the key areas of words, body and mind, along with a section of solutions and top tips. The lovely thing about Jacqui's writing is that, while she's a consummate professional and a visiting professor at INSEAD, her writing isn't dull or academic. It's easy to read and full of memorable stories from Jacqui and her clients' experience. In fact, I had to stop myself laughing out loud a few times as I read it, as I would have disturbed the other passengers on my flight! I would recommend this book to anyone who is serious about communications. I will be applying several of the tips to my own keynote speeches, safe in the knowledge that they are tried and tested, and that they will work for me as they have for so many others. Well done Jacqui!

Dr Penny Pullan,
keynote speaker and Director, Making Projects Work Ltd.

Executive Presentations guides you, step-by-step, to a nirvana where, when you speak, you are compelling, trustworthy, authentic and inspire confidence. Jacqui shows you how to combine the practical with the physical and emotional to become a leader people believe in. Buy it. Read it. Enjoy your success.

Joanne Gill,
Director, GLR Public Relations

Anyone who does any kind of presentation or public speaking knows just how difficult it is to deliver not only a memorable message but also one that engages with the audience. In this book, Jacqui has laid out strategies and concepts for delivering powerful and engaging presentation in the most straight forward and easily digestible way. This book will help you deliver your message with maximum effect. A must read for anyone looking to achieve impact and develop a powerful executive presence on any stage!

Griselda Togobo,
Entrepreneur, consultant, speaker, lecturer, author, CEO –
Forwardladies.com

Jacqui shares her experiences in her usual stylish and warm way – her book should be on everyone's reading list from 13 upwards. If you can write and present well, everything else is easy.

Meena Heath,
Founder, Global Leaders in Law

ACKNOWLEDGEMENTS

I T TAKES A lot of love to create a book and this is no exception. It has been given in the form of inspiration, encouragement, specialist advice, critical feedback, positive feedback, challenge and thoughtful comments. I am deeply grateful and would like to acknowledge three groups of people: those who have developed my expertise, those who've helped me grow as an author and my family.

My BBC colleagues from Newsroom South East: it's where my adventure in communication began. Amongst all the fun and deadlines I learnt a lot from colleagues. I have used many ideas and insights from broadcasting in my subsequent work in leadership development and in this book.

I am grateful to corporate clients and participants I have worked with at Crystal Business Coaching over the years on leadership development programmes, presentation skills courses, media training and executive coaching projects. Their questions, curiosity and courage have challenged me to keep on finding new and better ways to develop talented individuals.

The team of enthusiastic experts I have led at Crystal Business Coaching have been remarkable. Their specialist skills in training design, media coaching, voice coaching, image training and NLP techniques have created many unique and exciting training events that have thrilled our clients. The experts include Simon Nash, Cheryl Winter, Michaela Kennen, Carol Thompson, Sarah Simmons, Glen Oglaza, Judy Fearn, Dominique Douglas, Tim Friend and Jane Revell.

Thanks to my INSEAD colleague, Steve Knight, for putting me in touch with the Hudson Institute in Santa Barbara, where I trained as an executive coach. The Institute vi | *Executive Presentations*

transformed my thinking on adult learning and development. In executive coaching I gained a tool that is highly effective and a joy to use. The Hudson programme helped me grow as a person. I found useful blind spots to work on and re-discovered my jazz mode (that's the bit that doesn't have to be known or fully orchestrated – it can be created in the moment). I also found in the Phoenix Group a safe space to share hearts and minds on the most amazing learning journey.

Dr Penny Pullan is one of the main reasons this book has gone from interesting idea to printed page. A chance meeting with her at a women's network event in London's Docklands led me to join and win a Business Book Proposal Challenge (more of that in a minute). When I was struggling to write, my mastermind colleagues, Penny Pullan and Clare Painter, reminded me to write in my voice and that simple advice got me unstuck. Penny became my book buddy: we did daily check-ins and she reviewed many drafts – she has given me so much. I just knew there was something special about the lady with the lovely smile that I bumped into at HSBC Headquarters.

Alison Jones, owner of Practical Inspiration Publishing, is another author angel. She runs the excellent online 10-Day Business Book Proposal Challenge. As part of winning the challenge I was put on a six-week author boot camp that got me writing. She believed in this book even when I was wobbling. Thank you.

My Monday check-ins to the Facebook group created in the boot camp continued from first word to last. Knowing I had to tell the group SOMETHING at the start of every week was a useful motivator even when I stalled. Their responses and interest encouraged me.

A second Facebook group of friends, family and colleagues were also with me all the way. They read early drafts that were barely more than notes and their input meant a lot. They are

Monique Connor, Wim Dufourne, Susan Gellatly, Di Harper (lil' sis), Mike Normant and Dawn Rowley.

The biggest thanks must go to my family. I know writing the book sacrificed precious family time. Thank you Peter, Carla and Philip.

And finally, thanks to my parents Jasmine and Ralph: two humble Jamaicans who taught me how to love and dream.

CONTENTS

SECTION 1: WORDS

1 Begin powerfully 9
2 Reinforce ideas 25
3 Involve the audience 35
4 Be bold 45
5 End powerfully 55
6 When Jacqui met Harry or using scripts 61

SECTION 2: BODY

7 Vocal presence 69
8 Body language 87
9 Signature style 99
10 Headshots 117

SECTION 3: MIND

11 The attitude of gratitude 127
12 Self-coaching 137

SECTION 4: SOLUTIONS

13 Pitfalls and solutions 157
14 Nerves 179
15 Top tips 189

FIGURES

1 List of human feelings 11

2 Mapping emotional objectives..................13

3 Mind map..................37

4 Pyramid structure of 'How to Do a
Great Presentation' 40

5 BBC acronym 53

6 Prince Harry with Jacqui Harper..................61

7 Jacqui script with markups 65

8 Diaphragm breathing..................75

9 Vocal cords..................77

10 Colour groups and palettes..................105

11 Body shapes..................109

12 Headshots comparison 122

13 The Ladder of Inference 147

14 Productivity story 161

15 Vocal impact solutions..................169

16 Live graphics example..................176

17 Running order..................196

INTRODUCTION

Who is this book for?

- Do your presentations gain trust?
- Are your presentations always clear and compelling?
- Do your presentations inspire colleagues?
- Do your presentations enhance your corporate reputation?
- Are your presentations good enough to get you promoted?
- Do you speak with gravitas?
- Will your next role require strong executive presence?

If these questions raise issues you would like to address with practical, proven and innovative solutions, then this book is definitely for you. This is a powerful development tool for one of the most significant areas of competence for leaders: executive presence.

You might be an experienced and successful leader who wants to develop that specific area. You might be a newly promoted executive going into general management with new challenges and expectations. You might speak to international audiences. You might present at board meetings. You might be seeking new ideas for your presentations. You might be an emerging leader eager to support ambitions with stronger presentation skills.

This book is also a resource for those who focus on developing talent within their organisations. You might also be an executive coach supporting clients in issues to do with executive presence.

You might be on an exciting learning journey on an MBA programme or other business course, in which case this book will support you alongside your studies and ahead of your next role.

To all of you, welcome! I have written this book for you. You have been in my mind as I have written every word. You've helped me create a highly practical guide intended to inspire, challenge and instruct.

What exactly do I mean when I say 'presentation'?

Just for the sake of being crystal clear, executive presentations come in all shapes and sizes. I am of course including the set-piece conferences to several hundred people. I am also thinking of more intimate meetings with less than a hundred participants. Online presentations are very much in the mix, whether audio or video. Formal or informal board meetings are clearly places where executives are presenting ideas. Indeed, you can present information to just a few colleagues.

Why this book and why now?

We're all aware of just how volatile, uncertain, complex and ambiguous (VUCA) our working lives have become. In this environment an executive presentation is a critical form of business communication.

Corporations need to generate an awful lot of trust to address the challenges created in the VUCA world. Presenting ideas effectively can provide powerful shards of trust and authenticity that help create conditions for success within organisations.

Change can happen, teams can be built and strategy can come alive *when* people experience leaders with whom they feel deep trust and who express authentic, compelling and clear ideas. Presentations matter.

Executive presentations matter outside our organisations as well. Poor presentations can, and do, affect the value of a company. On the other hand, presentations that create trust and inspire confidence build brands and markets.

There are many excellent books on executive presence and on presentations. Most discuss the topics separately but this book links them, because effective presentations cannot happen without executive presence.

My approach in this book is that a humble presentation becomes the lion of business communication when you develop the three elements of presence: what we say, how we communicate with our body and how we think about ourselves and others.

Today, most business leaders are also speaking to audiences online, where it can be harder to generate the required level of trust. This book is highly relevant here in its focus on developing leadership presence that works across all modes of spoken communication. Leadership presence is a constant in many different contexts. This book also provides specific advice on the technical challenges of speaking online.

Corporations recognise that successful leaders must have executive presence. It's a competency that has become one of the most common reasons for hiring an executive coach. Evidence of executive presence is clearly seen in presentations, which is why it makes sense to do them well. Effective presentations build reputations and help people get promoted.

I've often heard the best CEOs described as 'Chief Engagement Officers'. Aspiring CEOs, however early in their career, will need to deliver presentations with executive presence to become engagement officers. This book will help you achieve just that.

Why me?

I was teaching at INSEAD one day when I heard an executive refer to me as 'the presentation doctor'. I burst out laughing. The nickname has since stuck and I don't mind it at all. It conveys my passion for helping people improve their presentations and also my expertise.

Alongside INSEAD, that passion is fulfilled through my company Crystal Business Coaching, which develops leaders from many industry sectors. I never fail to be thrilled at the end of a two-day course on presentation skills. There's always a moment on the second day when something clicks for each of the participants. You can see them literally growing in stature and confidence.

There's a different feeling of satisfaction when I am working as a communication coach. Here I am working with senior people who are grappling with a new role or focused on developing some aspect of their communication style. When it's one-to-one and a six-month engagement, you build a close relationship and cover so much ground. The depth of work and the long-lasting nature of the change are the best bits.

My expertise also comes from my own presentation experience. I do know exactly what it's like to speak in public under pressure. As an anchor on BBC News for many years it was a daily experience. Those years taught me a lot about how to manage pressure, how to think on my feet and how to communicate clearly.

I remember my first TV broadcast in the BBC studios in London. I remember walking down the stairs to the news studio full of fear and shaking. I remember the red light coming on above the camera and the director say, 'cue Jacqui!'. I managed to speak. I managed to get through the bulletin. I don't remember much else.

But the best lesson I got from TV was that presence and presenting skills can be improved quickly and to an accomplished extent. As you can tell from my story, my first broadcast was mediocre but that was just the beginning. I worked hard on getting better. I learned how to develop an authoritative presence.

My different roles mean I can share a unique and broad range of practical insights, techniques and tips to help you achieve mastery in executive presentations.

Away from work you will find me happily walking in the Yorkshire Dales or behind the lens of a camera.

I am proud to have been made an MBE by the Queen for services to the community. This was partly for running presentation training for inner-city children and using my presentation skills to promote mentoring for young people.

What will you gain from the book?

I have created a number of original tools and ideas to develop executive presence.

There's the BRIBE model. It's a five-step tool for making messages clear and compelling. It is an acronym I have used many times over the years. It enables speakers to create a presentation with maximum impact – every time. I have shared it with many executives and they just love it because it works and is easy to remember. I use it myself when I am speaking at conferences and other business meetings. It has saved me many times when asked to speak at the last minute. I know once I've got the beginning in order I can make the rest of the presentation work.

In the second section on how we communicate with our body I have developed two new strategies. The first is the concept of vocal presence, which explains how to speak with an authentic and competent voice. And there's the Signature Style framework for managing physical appearance to enhance presence.

Where do you start?

This book is about using presence to improve executive presentations. The ideas are organised in four sections: the first three sections focus on the three elements of presence – words, physical presence and state of mind. The fourth section looks at solutions to frequently raised presentation problems.

I have written the chapters so they are self-contained. You can just dip into the topic that interests you. Alternatively, you might want to read the BRIBE model in sequence. It's the first five chapters of the book and is all about making content clear and compelling. I would recommend reading the five chapters in sequence but it's your call.

For those of you that want to dip in and out of chapters, here's what you'll find in each chapter:

Chapter 1 is about making presentations robust from the very beginning. It shows you how to create the conditions for inspiration and motivation. It also provides proven techniques for capturing audience interest.

Chapter 2 is about getting your message across with maximum effect. Make your message memorable. Know how and where to re-state key points. There are also some handy words to know that help persuade an audience.

Chapter 3 discusses how to connect deeply with an audience. You'll learn the best way to use content to achieve that and the best physical techniques to work on.

Chapter 4 explores how to 'be bold' in order to deliver memorable messages. You'll see ways to make yourself and your ideas compelling. Graphics also get a makeover.

Chapter 5 ends the BRIBE model and is itself about ending a presentation. Here I deal with how to make sure a presentation stays strong to the very end. It also explains how to make sure the message is not missed.

Chapter 6 is where you rewrite scripts to make sure they sound natural and engaging. It takes you through the best way to rehearse with a script.

Chapter 7 is the first chapter in the Body section. It's about having a strong, authentic vocal presence. You'll learn the most useful exercises for achieving vocal competence.

Chapter 8 is rich in ideas for making your body language elevate your executive presence. There are techniques to reinforce credibility and boost rapport and impact.

Chapter 9 shares professional image techniques to give your presence the X factor.

Chapter 10 outlines the need for good headshots to support executive presence. You'll learn how to get the best out of a photoshoot and how to work with a photographer.

Chapter 11 starts the section on the Mind. In my view, you are what you think so positive thinking helps presence. The chapter shows how surprisingly valuable the daily practice of gratitude can be for leaders who want to excel.

Chapter 12 gives you tools to coach yourself to improve presence. You'll learn how to prepare your mind for success, how to unravel thoughts that hold you back and a new technique for rehearsals.

Chapter 13 is the first chapter on Solutions. I tackle some of the issues executives have raised on my courses and explain in detail how to avoid major pitfalls.

Chapter 14 is my favourite. It is entirely devoted to the subject of nerves. I have interviewed a range of leaders and experts to get their advice. This chapter has breadth, and the answers provide fresh insights and inspiring ideas.

Chapter 15 closes the book with my top ten tips. They address the common challenges for speakers and are designed to give you a boost as you make your journey to mastery.

Further resources

This book along with extra resources at www. crystalbusinesscoaching.com aims to inspire and inform you with practical ideas and tips you can start using straight away.

Do let me know how you get on. You can interact with me and other readers on the site.

I wish you great success as you develop your presence and give authentic presentations that gain deep trust.

Chapter 1

BEGIN POWERFULLY

B EGIN A PRESENTATION powerfully and you have a huge advantage. A weak start on the other hand can be very hard to turn around. This chapter is about achieving that advantage with effective ways to connect quickly and deeply to an audience.

This chapter is also the first of five on making the most of your message. I've created a tool called BRIBE to help you communicate clear and compelling ideas. BRIBE is an easy-to-remember acronym and each letter represents a topic covered in this and subsequent chapters. The acronym is explained below.

BRIBE model

B = Begin Powerfully
R = Reinforce Ideas
I = Involve the Audience
B = Be Bold
E = End Powerfully

Preview

This chapter shows four ways to make the strongest start to an executive presentation:
- The emotional objective
- The information objective
- The preview
- The Hook

The emotional objective

> I've learned that people will forget what you said, people
> will forget what you did, but people will never forget how
> you made them feel.
>
> *Maya Angelou*[1]

Executive speakers would do well to follow the wise words
of writer Maya Angelou. Instead, too often people start
preparing a presentation by focusing on the objective. This
usually means the information objective of the presentation:
the point or ideas they want the audience to take away.

The information objective is important but I would
encourage a slightly different starting point. If Maya Angelou
is right and ultimately what's remembered is how you make an
audience feel, then start with the emotional objective. By that
I mean think about what you want the audience to *feel* when
you've finished speaking. Do you want them to feel excited,
uncomfortable, comfortable, reassured, curious, reflective,
encouraged? Be clear about the precise emotional response
you want to elicit.

Alongside this, consider ways to evoke those emotions.
At your disposal are the words you choose, storytelling, the
structure of the presentation, the themes, the slide deck, your
voice, body language, facial expressions and your appearance.
All these points are discussed throughout this book. Points
about content are covered in chapters on the BRIBE model.
There's more information on how to use your body to
communicate your message on page 87.

The focus on working with an emotional objective can
help create a deep connection with an audience. It establishes
the kind of rapport that makes an audience more likely to
want to listen to what you have to say.

This technique of using emotional objectives in public
speaking has been around since ancient times. The Greek

philosopher Aristotle is a well-known exponent of it. In his book *The Art of Rhetoric* he identifies three tools for effective speech: argument, character and emotion. When speaking in public, Aristotle says:

> One should lead the listener to emotions. These are pity and indignation, anger and hatred and envy, jealousy and strife.[2]

Later in this chapter, on page 22, we return to Aristotle's ideas on public speaking.

Today, many would identify slightly different fundamental human emotions: happiness, sadness, fear, anger, surprise, disgust and trust. It is certainly possible to use some of these emotions in executive presentations but it feels a bit limiting to me. When I am speaking at conferences I like to have more nuanced emotional objectives available to me so I turn to feelings, sometimes called compounds of emotions.[3]

When teaching at INSEAD I often show participants a chart listing human *feelings* and I encourage them to select the feeling(s) most relevant to the executive presentation they are creating. I remind them that there is one feeling relevant to all presentations: trust. See Figure 1 for others.

Glad	Hopeful	Able	Curious
Happy	Expectant	Confident	Good
Delighted	Relieved	Powerful	Great
Joyful	Satisfied	Interested	Compassion
Elated	Certain	Awe	Sympathy
Thrilled	Assured	Inspired	Empathy
Comfortable	Eager	Uncomfortable	Annoyed
Excited	Enthusiastic	Nervous	Shocked
Positive	Concerned	Thoughtful	Unhappy
Impressed	Challenged	Cheerful	Pride

Figure 1: List of human feelings

Without doubt the most effective way of achieving emotional objectives in presentations is through storytelling. Our brains just love stories. A good story activates many parts of the brain, releases oxytocin, makes us more empathic and more co-operative. Go to page 160 for insights on telling good stories in business meetings.[4]

Mapping emotions

Some people find it useful to have one overarching emotional objective for an entire presentation. Others like the idea of mapping specific emotional objectives to different parts of the presentation. For example, you might want surprise at the beginning of a presentation; reassurance in the middle; and excitement as the emotional objective at the end.

Figure 2 shows an emotional map of a lecture I give on executive presence. It shows the emotions I'm focused on and the ways I choose to generate them. As an exercise, I often ask participants to scrutinise my opening speech to them and identify the emotional objectives. Thankfully, they've always identified the emotions I intended!

Element of presentation	Emotional objective	Ways to generate the emotions
Beginning	Trust	Tell them a short story of my lifelong love affair with communication – to understand my expertise and passion for the subject.
Beginning	Enthusiasm	Smile and speak with vocal energy, facial animation and gestures.

Middle	Thoughtful	Give the audience new ways to think about the structure of a presentation by sharing the BRIBE model.
Middle	Thoughtful	Ask questions – both real and rhetorical.
Middle	Surprise	Use unexpected examples to illustrate ideas. For example, I sometimes show a short video of international rapper Kanye West accepting a music award because it is an exceptional example of how to end a speech. There's more discussion of this example on page 58.
End	Inspiration	Close class with an inspiring quote. One of my favourites is an extract from the inaugural speech of the late Nelson Mandela. He in turn borrowed it from American writer and women's advocate, Marianne Williamson. It talks beautifully about letting go of fear and owning your power and talent. I never tire of reading it. Go to the link to read in full. www.goodreads.com/quotes/928-our-deepest-fear-is-not-that-we-are-inadequate-our

Figure 2: Mapping emotional objectives

The information objective or WIIFM

We move from discussing the emotional objective to the information objective. I have been using WIIFM (pronounced 'wiff-mm') for so long that I cannot remember where I first came across it. It simply stands for **What's In It For Me**. The 'me' in this instance is the audience not the speaker.

This is about audience advocacy. It's about putting yourself into the minds of an audience. It's about giving an audience a clear understanding of what they will gain from your presentation and why it is so relevant to them. They need to know they will get something of high value in return for giving you their time and attention.

I encourage you to be explicit about the WIIFM and to deliver it within three or so minutes of starting a presentation. This timing can be extended slightly if you are speaking for a longer period of time – but not by much. If you take too long making clear what's in it for the audience, you risk them disengaging from your speech while they figure out for themselves what's in it for them. In the early moments of a presentation it is instinctive to wonder where a speaker is going: if that curiosity is satisfied in good time it's a promising start.

The WIIFM is slightly different from the agenda although it can be revealed as part of the agenda. The WIIFM is more a global perspective of a presentation or the big picture. If the audience take one thing away from your presentation that clearly benefits them – what is it? Be rigorous in identifying the WIIFM. A well-chosen WIIFM will give your audience a powerful reason to listen to you.

The WIIFM is also a useful editing tool when you are in the preparation stage of your presentation. Knowing the ultimate purpose of the presentation, from the audience perspective, means you can focus ruthlessly on content that serves the purpose.

A good example of WIIFM is Sheryl Sandberg's TED Talk about getting more women into leadership. It's a 20-minute presentation and she delivers the WIIFM within the first few minutes. Her WIIFM is the specific things audience members can do in their day-to-day lives to address the lack of women in leadership roles across the world. She's clear the WIIFM is nothing to do with corporate policy but is explicitly about personal actions.

To watch the presentation in full go to the following link: www.youtube.com/watch?v=18uDutylDa4

Another good example of WIIFM is Laura Sicola's interesting TEDx Talk on vocal executive presence. Her audience learn early on what they can get from her talk: vocal strategies to reinforce a message and to establish the leadership image you want.

The link for that presentation is: www.youtube.com/watch?v=02EJ1IdC6tE

The preview

The preview builds on the foundations of the emotional objective and the WIIFM. Its function is to give further clarity to ideas and keep the audience engaged. From observing many presentations I would say the quickest way to lose an audience is to start a speech with a lack of clarity. It takes a lot of work to rescue things if the audience don't know what you're talking about and why.

The preview effectively fills in the blanks that might be created by the objectives. The objectives are by their nature general, global points and it won't be long before an audience needs to know more. The preview gives the audience an understanding of how you've organised your thinking: the structure, the sequence, the approach. It gives the audience information on what else they can expect from you.

Many people choose an agenda slide to explain the preview. Often this does the job well and takes the form of a list with bullet points. This format is fine and is one to keep in the portfolio. I would also encourage a little more fresh thinking on the agenda.

It can be delivered effectively without any slides at all. I call this style of speaking 'naked' because it can feel like speaking without 'protection': it can generate a feeling of vulnerability in a presentation setting. The good news though is that it will make you work hard at being crystal clear in your messaging.

For more about the power of naked presentations, see 'The tips' section on page 197.

But the best bit is this style enables you to deeply engage the audience at a crucial time in the speech; that is, when you are establishing connection. Slides can be distracting and interfere with the delicate relationship-building taking place.

If you're not quite ready for no slides then making slides work better is a good option. Keeping words to a minimum will help. For example, having no more than four words per line helps the audience scan the slide quickly. That way the audience spend minimum time with their attention away from listening to the speaker. There are more ideas for great graphics on page 48.

A picture-only preview can be effective providing the image is clear, has impact and is totally relevant to the points you're making. Having an image-only preview means the audience is less distracted and, more than that, it means the audience *has* to listen more closely to understand what the picture means and where the presentation is going.

The Hook

So what's the Hook? It's what a speaker says or does to get attention to hook the audience into a presentation. Sometimes it's called the go-getter. In addition to getting our attention, an effective Hook will help the audience connect to the theme or subject of the presentation. I have never tried using a Hook that doesn't have that dual function.

The Hook comes in many forms and for me is an exciting aspect of a presentation. Devising an effective Hook is often deeply frustrating and exhilarating. The frustration comes from the process of considering lots of different types of Hooks and feeling that for one reason or another they don't quite work. The exhilaration happens when you find the Hook that is just right for the presentation and the audience. That light bulb moment thrills me every time.

I want to spend a little time highlighting the strengths of different Hooks. I'll concentrate on:

- Quotes
- Powerful images
- Surprise
- You
- Curiosity

Quotes

Quotes are popular Hooks. They can be words from a famous speaker or a business leader, or quotes from a poem or literature. Shakespeare is a popular choice in executive presentations because his plays are so well known and themes such as power, leadership, challenge, conflict, adversity and hope are ripe for visionary presentations.

A source for useful quotes is: www.greatest-inspirational-quotes.com

After a quick browse of the internet here are a few quotes I like:

- I would like to be remembered as someone who did the best she could with the talent she had: *JK Rowling*

- Good business is the best art of all: *Andy Warhol*
- Instead of thinking out of the box – get rid of the box: *Deepak Chopra*
- Being a good human being is good business: *Paul Hawken*
- I choose a lazy person to do a hard job because a lazy person will find an easy way to do it: *Bill Gates*
- Don't be pushed by your problems. Be led by your dreams: *Ralph Waldo Emerson.*

See Chapter 13 for tips on making the most of quotes (see page 164).

Powerful images

I've already suggested using images for previewing a presentation. Pictures also make great Hooks. One of the most impressive pictures I came across was from a participant at the British Foreign Office. The speaker was delivering a presentation about political instability in a particular country. He started his presentation with a huge, high-resolution image of a protester about to be struck violently in the head by a soldier.

The image of the vicious strike was frozen in mid-action and drew gasps of horror from the audience. Our brains couldn't help taking us to the grim inevitability of what happened next when the soldier's baton cracked the man's skull. The Hook got the audience's attention. The image made us want to learn more about the reasons for the violence and so we were more than ready for the political analysis that followed. The picture prevented the speech from being too conceptual.

Surprise

I recall a speaker whose purpose was to get staff to change wasteful practices in the workplace. The speaker scanned the room dramatically, paused and then set light to a real £5 note. It was only alight for a few moments and I am sure Health and Safety were not aware and would not have been amused. Nevertheless, this surprising start was a powerful way to connect the audience to the theme of wasting money.

Surprise is a powerful human emotion that can be highly effective in executive presentations. It works so well because it motivates people to pay attention. Our brain gets to work straight away trying to figure out what is happening and what it means. As Dan and Chip Heath neatly note, our brain is like a guessing machine constantly using patterns and experiences to predict what will happen. A surprise interrupts the guessing machine.

When our guessing machines fail, surprise grabs our attention so that we can repair them for the future.[5]

Surprise can be achieved in many ways: dramatic, subtle or anywhere in-between. We're really only limited by our imagination.

A more subtle example. Take something familiar and add something surprising to it. Many people know the phrase 'I came, I saw, I conquered' written by the powerful Roman General, Julius Caesar and used in Shakespeare's *As You Like It*.

The quote could be re-used in a presentation with the words 'I came, I saw, I cried'. As we cry in pain or from happiness, the quote can be the start of a discussion about business performance that causes concern or brings joy. The trick is making sure the adapted version is clearly linked to the original.[6]

Another example of this is the headline 'The Good, The Bad and The Prezza'. It's obviously derived from the Clint Eastwood western, *The Good, The Bad and The Ugly*. What makes this particularly amusing to UK audiences is that 'Prezza' is the nickname of former British deputy Prime

Minister Lord Prescott. He has many qualities but would never be mistaken for the Hollywood actor. In fact, the story following the headline was a humorous newspaper apology for captioning Lord Prescott as Clint Eastwood.[7] News headlines can be a rich source of ideas for business presentations.

A surprising Hook I came across was at a travel industry presentation. The presentation was about the country of Bali and the speaker's Hook was the sense of smell. He had the aroma of neroli (orange blossom) wafting throughout the meeting room as he started speaking. I have never forgotten it. In fact, it started my interest in aromatherapy!

You

How you show up as a speaker can sometimes be the best Hook for an executive presentation. You can use your presence to deliver a powerful beginning and it doesn't always need to be all bells and whistles to be effective.

I recently saw a speaker in Santa Barbara start his presentation in the most unassuming way. He stood at the front of the conference room while participants took to their seats. He looked relaxed and smiling. There was something else about his presence I couldn't quite identify. My best guess was that he seemed 'peaceful'. Anyway, there were no slide decks or handouts. As he was about to start he *sat down* on a chair. I was curious. In a deeply expressive voice he started speaking. What followed was one of the best business seminars I have ever attended: engaging, challenging, exciting, funny and richly informative. Somehow we knew we were in for a treat from the understated Hook.

The speaker was Russ Hudson, a world expert on *The Enneagram*. If you've not come across this tool it's a good one for speakers who want to become more self-aware and more present. At its simplest there's a test you can do to understand your personality type but it is way more than that.

If you're seeking a strong impact, low-frills Hook let me introduce BLAB. It helps speakers get control at the beginning of their presentation when nerves are most likely to kick in. It forces you to slow down, breathe deeply to fuel the voice and engage eye contact.

BLAB

When I'm teaching this I get my participant to start 'off stage' (at the side of the room) and walk to the centre of the room. It's more effective if the pace of walking is measured, purposeful and energetic.

I insist there is no speaking while walking as I see too many instances of speakers diminishing their impact on entrance. When you arrive at the podium you pause and BLAB. That is, you take a full diaphragm breath – B, look into the audience and around the room – L, pause and – A then begin speaking – B. It's summarised below:

BLAB
- Breathe
- Look
- And
- Begin

This deceptively simple technique makes such a dramatic difference to my participants. It's quite remarkable. Indeed, BLAB is so fundamental to making an executive presentation start well that I would argue it is actually best practice for starting *any* presentation.

When you want to be a more dynamic Hook, focus on presence. Pay attention to what the audience experience of you before you've said a single word. This means making use of body language, gestures, facial expressions, your energy level and your breathing. For more on body language, see Chapter 8.

What you wear and your overall appearance can transform your impact. As always it's about detail: accessories; grooming; the quality, cut and styling of clothes. And colour. Colour is virtually the first thing an audience notices when you walk on stage. Colours can signal power, authority and confidence. Chapter 9 on Signature Style shows how to make your appearance an asset in an executive presentation. See page 99.

Curiosity

This is one of my favourite Hooks because it's so simple and so effective. If you get it right it piques interest and is quick and efficient at connecting to the core message of a presentation. You can generate curiosity in many ways including by asking a question, holding a prop or showing a slide with an unexplained statistic, fact or picture.

For example, I deliver a course on presentations for a French multinational company. The first slide my participants see is a painting from ancient times. Its focus is a distinguished-looking guy in a flowing robe and I ask the class to guess who he is and why he's so important to our training session. Occasionally someone guesses his name correctly. Very few know why he's relevant to business meetings but with such highly competitive business leaders in the room the energy rises while participants make smart guesses about the mystery man.

Once we've identified that the man in the picture is in fact Aristotle, the Ancient Greek philosopher and scientist, it's easy to bring in his highly relevant ideas on the art of public speaking. He tells us that great presentations happen when three things are present: pathos, logos and ethos.

- Pathos – an emotional connection between speaker and audience
- Logos – a sequence of ideas that is well structured and well crafted
- Ethos – a speaker with a positive and credible presence.

The very process of getting participants to guess means I am engaging their minds and drawing them into the presentation. It's the knowledge gap created by the mystery man that makes curiosity so effective. We just have an irrepressible intellectual need to know the answer and close open patterns.[8]

Another variant of curiosity is mystery. If curiosity is about creating a short-lived knowledge gap then mystery is an extended gap. It's a bit like a murder mystery where information gradually unfolds and you don't know the full picture until the end. It's probably one to use sparingly in business presentations but it can certainly be used.

Summary

- The emotional objective provides a vital connection to an audience and enables influence
- The information objective – WIIFM – needs to be clear and highly relevant to the audience and it needs to be delivered early
- The preview helps those listening understand where arguments are going and keeps the audience on board
- The Hook has many forms: the right Hook will deliver a powerful start.

Reflective questions

- Which emotional objectives are relevant to your presentation?
- Which is the most important?
- How will you achieve the emotional objectives?
- How effectively are you delivering the emotional objectives?
- What issues or factors affect your choice of WIIFM?
- How soon does your audience hear the WIIFM?

- How clearly stated is your WIIFM?
- Which style of preview best suits your presentation and audience?
- Are you ready to go 'naked' with the preview?
- Is the preview clear and succinct?
- Does your explanation of the preview make the audience want to know more?
- What's the best Hook for your presentation?

Chapter 2

REINFORCE IDEAS

THIS IS THE second of five chapters on making the most of your message. I've created a tool called BRIBE to communicate clear and compelling ideas. BRIBE is an easy-to-remember acronym with each letter representing a topic on presentation content. The acronym is explained below.

BRIBE model

B = Begin Powerfully
R = Reinforce Ideas
I = Involve the Audience
B = Be Bold
E = End Powerfully

Preview

This chapter covers a technique that's consistently underused in executive presentations: reinforcing ideas. It discusses the following points:

- Repetition
- Themes
- The News Model
- Q&A
- The Persuaders

I often wonder why repetition isn't used to its full advantage in executive presentations. Maybe it's because people feel that once they've said a point the audience knows it and there's no need to re-state it. That thinking is *so* wrong. In reality it's difficult to get people to remember what we say.

Regardless of the skill of the speaker, no audience will pay attention 100% of the time. Individuals are bound to drift, even if momentarily. 'Naked' presentations, without slides and other speaker support, are particularly challenging as audience retention can be as low as 10%.[9] The powerful answer lies in reinforcing ideas to help listeners remember the important things we've said. I think of it as insurance policy for messages.

The first step is clarifying the core theme or message of your presentation. A useful way to do this is to take a look at the entire content of the presentation and summarise it in a few words. Journalists do this all the time when they give stories a short title called a slug.

For example, my first byline as a journalist at *The Oakland Tribune* in California was a profile of an unusual entrepreneur. She sold glamorous, sexy evening dresses and was a Buddhist nun who used the profits from the business to fund religious training schools in India. The slug for that story was 'Designer Nun'. With the slug defined I found it rather easy to identify the key points of the story and subsequently write the article.

However you arrive at the key point(s) of your presentation, the next step is to choose the most relevant reinforcing technique.

When I am teaching this topic I do a simple word exercise to illustrate the main ways to emphasise ideas. I read out a list of 25 'random' words and then ask participants to write down the words they find most memorable. They usually remember the words that have been intentionally highlighted or have a prominent position such as:

- The first and last words
- Unusual words
- Words emphasised with gestures
- Thematic words – similar or related words
- Repeated words.

Repetition

Repetition is just so effective. It is literally saying the same words or phrase several times. Thankfully, there are other ways to repeat a core message. For example, putting a strapline on all slides in a deck works well; you can also show a video or written information that re-states a key point.

Or, you can highlight a single, significant item and repeat it. There's a really good example of this technique in the track '19' by British recording artist Paul Hardcastle. The number 19 is repeated throughout the track and it refers to the average age of American soldiers fighting in the Vietnam War. Be warned it looks like, and is, an 80s video. Despite its age it illustrates the technique well. Take a look at the video link: www.youtube.com/watch?v=b3LdMAqUMnM

Using this technique in an executive presentation might need some modification but the result could be rather striking.

An outstanding example of repetition occurs in the speech given by Martin Luther King Junior the day before his assassination. It's sometimes called the 'I've been to the mountain top' speech.[10]

Towards the end of the speech, Martin Luther King Junior recalls how ten years earlier he was stabbed by a woman and came close to death. While recovering in hospital he singled out one of the letters he received.

It was from a high school student who'd learned in the media of the attack on Dr King. She was struck by a comment in the paper that if Dr King had sneezed he would have died. She simply says she is so happy he did not sneeze. The rest of the speech picks up on this phrase. Indeed, 'If I had sneezed' is repeated six more times. Dr King skilfully uses each repetition of the phrase to recall a different milestone in the U.S. civil rights movement in the ten years since the stabbing. The phrase is mentioned in three different contexts: as part of a story in *The New York Times*, a letter from a schoolgirl and an expression of Dr King's own feelings. It is an incredibly moving speech and a superb use of repetition.

Again, the business equivalent would probably need adapting but it could work well in a presentation where inspiration is the primary purpose.

Have a listen. The link is www.youtube.com/watch?v=pqPsykBx3sc

Location, location, location. Education, education, education. These are examples of repetition called *epizeuxis*. The first example is the memorable title of a popular TV show in the UK and it's also a familiar phrase uttered by real estate agents. *Education, education, education* is taken from a conference speech by Tony Blair just before he became British Prime Minister. He was emphasising his priority in government if elected. The speech is still remembered today and in particular the repeated words.

The technique of saying the same word three times comes from Ancient Greek rhetoric.[11] Amazingly, epizeuxis creates a pattern of words in your head that seems impossible to remove. This is one to use sparingly but in the right place could be potent.

Themes

I mentioned earlier the word exercise that I use with participants. I scatter thematic words throughout my list of words. For example, I sometimes use the words *hair, hairstyle* and *hairbrush*. People don't always remember all three words but they almost always remember the hair theme and a couple of the hair words.

The research professor Brené Brown gives an excellent example of how to reinforce themes in her TED Talk 'The Power of Vulnerability'. The link is: www.ted.com/talks/brene_brown_on_vulnerability

Although she calls the talk 'The Power of Vulnerability' I would say the theme is connection and disconnection. She argues that connecting deeply to our selves and the world around us requires us to embrace our vulnerability in order to feel joy, gratitude and happiness. Disconnection, on the other hand, from pain in our lives creates many serious problems.

How does she reinforce the theme of connection? With striking images. One of the early slides is a close up of a child's hand protectively held in the palm of an adult. It's a tender image and portrays connection perfectly. Also it's hard not to notice the racial impact of the image. Both child and adult are black and even in the 21st century this seems to stand out because the context is universal not racial. The image definitely attracts attention.

A second striking image that reinforces the theme of connection is of red hearts. Nothing striking about that you might say. Well, the picture is a close up of hanging ornamental hearts that look like they might be made of red glass. It's a fresh image of a familiar icon that represents connection.

The image reappears in the presentation in even greater magnification and this time you can't see the heart shape, just the transparent red glass. It's used as a background with the words *courage, compassion* and *connection* superimposed: the visual is simple and arresting.

The other way Brown reinforces her theme is with storytelling. She relates an amusing first encounter between herself and her therapist. The story starts with struggle and resistance. Later Brown reveals that she had a breakdown before learning to lean into her own vulnerability.

The position of the story is effective in joining the two halves of the presentation. The story reinforces all the early points about understanding the concept of connection. The story also prepares the audience for the second half of the presentation that focuses on solutions and how to achieve connection.

Incidentally, Brown's thoughts on connection are useful reflections for anyone giving executive presentations. I believe the depth of connection a speaker has to an audience is directly related to how the speaker embraces their own vulnerability.

The News Model

The structure of a news bulletin offers a simple template for where to reinforce ideas. The structure is typically:

- Headlines
- Stories
- Break – recap or still to come
- Stories
- Recap

The elements of a bulletin correspond quite neatly to a presentation. The headlines at the start of a bulletin are similar to the introduction of a presentation. The headlines tell the audience the key stories in the bulletin. The introduction to a presentation lets the audience know the main themes.

Individual news stories are similar to key points in a presentation. They are the place where ideas are explained.

Halfway through a bulletin, audiences get a breather. The anchor either recaps the top stories or does 'still to come'. That is, the anchor lets the audience know the main stories that will feature in the rest of the bulletin.

I really like the idea of introducing a breather into presentations. It gives the audience an opportunity to process what they've heard and breaks up the pace of the presentation. It also gives the speaker an opportunity to re-state the themes of the presentation.

The recap at the end of a bulletin gives the audience a final opportunity to hear what's going on in the world. The conclusion of a presentation gives the audience one last chance to understand the main points and ideas.

The news template brings to mind the well-known advice (but not always followed) for reinforcing ideas: tell them what you're going to tell them, tell them, then tell them what you just told them.

Q&A

This is the ideal place to support ideas. First there's the introduction to the Q&A. Here you can remind an audience of the main points they've heard in the preceding presentation.

When taking questions there's a simple formula to make answers clear and emphatic: PEP.

P = is the point that answers the question

E = is the example that explains the point

P = is the main point re-stated or summarised.

Use the conclusion of the Q&A as the last opportunity to reinforce your theme or key point. There's more information on making the most of Q&A on page 190.

The Persuaders

It's a good idea to have in your presentation vocabulary some of the best words for persuading people. I call them them *The Persuaders*. They're not new but they are effective. Use them to reinforce your ideas. They are:

Discovery

Guarantee

Love

Proven

Results

Save

Easy

Health

Money

New

Safety

You[12]

Summary

Repetition is a highly effective tool for supporting important ideas in a presentation. When used skilfully it can help inspire audiences. Themes can come alive with striking images and storytelling. The News Model provides a simple template to reinforce ideas at the beginning, middle and end of a presentation. Q&A provides fertile opportunities for re-stating ideas and themes. Make use of persuasive words as you get your message across.

Reflective questions

- What slug summarises your presentation?
- What points need repeating?
- What other techniques will help reinforce ideas?
- Where are the most useful places in the presentation to reinforce points?
- What are the themes in your presentation?
- Which tools will help your theme the most?
- What ideas do you want to highlight in Q&A?
- What final point do you want your audience to hear when you close the Q&A?

Chapter 3

INVOLVE THE AUDIENCE

THIS IS THE third of five chapters on making the most of your message. I've created a tool called BRIBE to communicate clear and compelling ideas. BRIBE is an easy-to-remember acronym with each letter representing a topic on presentation content. The acronym is explained below.

BRIBE model

B = Begin Powerfully
R = Reinforce Ideas
I = Involve the Audience
B = Be Bold
E = End Powerfully

Preview

I remember settling into my chair as a speaker walked towards a podium. I had been looking forward to the presentation for weeks and now the wait was over. As the speaker began he was looking closely at his notes. And that's where his eyes stayed – for the entire presentation. He did not look up once, even as his audience shuffled restlessly. Time passed very slowly and it was hard to connect to the speaker or his ideas.

Things would have been so different if the speaker understood that presentations are binary events: speaker and audience must be involved to achieve success. The techniques that really bring an audience into a presentation are:

- Meaningful eye contact
- Content that doesn't overload an audience – Magic 7
- Clearly organised ideas using the pyramid structure
- Stories that connect audiences to the subject and the speaker

This chapter explains these ideas.

Eye contact

Probably the most powerful tool for involvement is eye contact. When there's effective eye contact, you know it and your audience knows it. The only problem is that speakers often feel uncomfortable looking directly at people in an audience.

There may be good reasons for the discomfort including cultural practices. Direct eye contact in some cultures (Native Americans, some Asian countries) is perceived as disrespectful or hostile. Even within cultures that use very direct eye contact (Middle Eastern, Hispanic, French) if it is held for too long a time it can be seen as aggressive or intrusive.

I was raised in the UK by parents from Jamaica and I know the message received in my childhood was that it was disrespectful to look directly into the eyes of adults. It is something I had to work on consciously in my early adult life in my role as a business reporter.

Other barriers to making valuable eye contact include the physical space in a venue. In very large auditoriums the distance can make it virtually impossible to make real eye contact.

My earlier story about the speaker looking down at notes implies the barriers to making eye contact were personality and/or poor speaker support. Reading scripts can be especially difficult for speakers wanting to maintain eye contact. So let's turn to solutions. There's a helpful chapter on how to present well with scripts on page 61. I would also recommend mind maps to significantly increase eye contact.

Eye contact: Mind maps

Mind maps are well worth exploring as speaker prompts. You do need to rehearse the content quite thoroughly to get the best results. They help us speak in a relaxed, natural style which is highly engaging. I often use them when speaking at conferences. I like the fact that they are quick and easy to prepare. They are also brilliant for adapting to last-minute time changes. If you suddenly find yourself with less speaking time, it's really easy to drop key points or examples.

There are a number of different software tools to write mind maps on electronic devices including *Mindmeister* and *iMindMap*. For a good review of mind mapping software go to: https://business.tutsplus.com/articles/best-mind-mapping-software-tools--cms-29581

I confess, in this instance I am old school. I just love creating mind maps with brightly coloured felt tip pens. The physical act of drawing a mind map with my hands helps me process and internalise the content of my presentation.

So how do you create a mind map for a presentation? Take a look at Figure 3 and the notes:

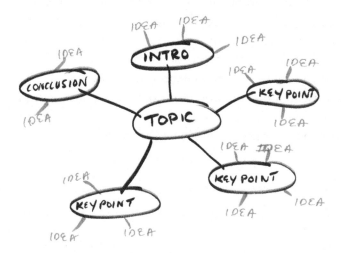

Figure 3: Mind map

Let's say you have five elements to your presentation: introduction, three key points and a conclusion.

1. In the centre of a blank sheet of A4 paper (landscape) draw an ellipse (egg-shaped circle). Inside the shape write the topic of the presentation – one word if you can.

2. Draw five lines radiating from the central shape. Draw an ellipse at the end of these lines. Label each shape with key words. Each key word corresponds to a main point of the presentation.

3. Let's start with the first key word (at midday). Assuming it's the intro and you have three ideas to explain, then draw three lines from the shape and at the end of each line write the idea (one word if possible). That word is your prompt to explain the supporting idea.

4. Continue to capture the content of your entire presentation going clockwise around the mind map.

If you are using a mind map as a speaker prompt, keep it really clear and easy to read so you don't have to look down for long. As I said before you *must* rehearse. During rehearsal you may discover some of the words you've chosen are not the best prompts for you. You will know when you've got the right word as it easily triggers the ideas you want to explain.

If you are new to mind maps it might be worth staggering their use in a presentation. For example, to start with just do the introduction using the mind map or one of the key points. A few more thoughts on using mind maps.

Tips

*   Use capital letters – easier to read in a live presentation
*   Use one or two words – keeps the mind map uncluttered and is easier to remember

- Use colour. Use a different colour for each key word and its supporting ideas
- Draw simple images – helps with remembering the point
- Use delivery prompts – e.g. an asterisk could signal the next slide. An exclamation mark could signal a pause.

If you're not sure about mind maps you can always work with bullet points on cue cards. You can adapt the bullet points in many ways to make them easier to read while speaking. Use colour, capital letters, key words and wide spacing to help.

Overload: Magic 7

Overloading audiences with information happens too often in business presentations and leads to disengagement. One of the best tools for keeping audiences involved is Magic 7. It refers to a theory by psychologist George Miller often called *The Magical Number Seven, Plus or Minus Two*. He said that we can hold seven random items in short-term memory at any one time. That number can go up to nine or reduce to five.[13]

When we apply this idea to presentations, the items are the key points. Grouping ideas around seven key points works fine. If you want to be cautious five key points avoids any chance of overload.

Clearly organised ideas: The pyramid structure

Barbara Minto's excellent *Pyramid Principle* is a tool for communicating ideas that audiences find easy to follow.[14] When ideas flow well the audience stays with the speaker. I tend to use the pyramid principle after brainstorming to tidy up my thinking and the structure. You might like to know that I have used the pyramid structure shown in Figure 4 to write this book.

The idea of the pyramid structure is that it follows how our brain processes information. The brain likes patterns, systems, things in categories. The pyramid structure puts ideas into simple pyramids with a headline at the top and supporting points at the bottom of the pyramid.

See Figure 4 for my presentation titled 'How to Do a Great Presentation' in pyramid format. Note the second line below the title is called the keyline and it identifies the two main arguments of the presentation. In my case a great presentation is all about 1) the message and 2) the messenger.

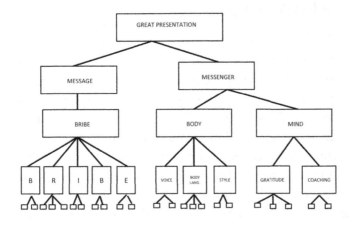

Figure 4: Pyramid structure of 'How to Do a Great Presentation'

When you look at the graphic in Figure 4 there are pyramids all over the place. The big pyramid is the shape of the overall graphic. 'Great Presentation' is at the top of the pyramid and the blank boxes on the bottom line are the base of the pyramid. These boxes represent single ideas that help explain what makes a great presentation.

There's another pyramid formed by the top three boxes: 'Great Presentation' is the top of the pyramid and on the keyline are the boxes 'Message' and 'Messenger', which form the base of the pyramid. The keyline boxes answer the question implied by the box above. For example, if the question is how do you do a great presentation, the answer is focus on the message and the messenger.

There's a pyramid formed under the 'Messenger' box. If the question is what can a messenger do to achieve a great presentation, then the answer is pay attention to your body and your mind.

Under the box labelled 'Body' is another triangle formed with the boxes 'Voice', 'Body Language' and 'Style'. If the question is how can your body help with a great presentation, the answer is work on your voice, your body language and your style.

A couple more points on using the pyramid structure. Any box in the pyramid explains the one above that it is linked to.

The pyramid principle helps with putting ideas into the best order. The horizontal line with BRIBE enables ideas to be easily grouped together. The sequence of letters of the acronym dictates the order. However, if we move across to the keyline box 'Messenger', below it is the box 'Body' and then 'Mind'. I've chosen to discuss ideas about the body before ideas about the mind. This is because my discussion on the body is highly practical and full of doing things while the ideas about the mind are more reflective and felt better suited towards the end of the book. Do scrutinise the order in which you explain ideas.

Barbara Minto summarises neatly four ways to group ideas.

- Deductively (major premise, minor premise, conclusion)
- Chronologically (first, second, third)
- Structurally (Boston, New York, Washington)
- Comparatively (first most important, second most important etc.).[15]

Stories that connect

Once you've got the structure sorted it's time to make the content come alive. I've already referred to stories powering up the beginning of a presentation. I'm returning to storytelling again because it's all but guaranteed to involve an audience and influence them. As coaching expert Jenny Rogers says:

> Stories appeal to the limbic system, the emotional centre of the brain and the seat of all our decision-making.[16]

To really leverage the power of a story there are a few things to get right. An effective story communicates a significant idea. We all know the three elements to a story: beginning, middle and end. The beginning establishes the setting for the central character. The middle has an important moment or trigger and the end contains the learning or conclusion.

Here's the breakdown of a story I sometimes share when introducing myself to groups.

The beginning

The story is about an important moment in the life of a ten-year-old child. The story takes place in a classroom where a teacher asks various ten year olds to read out an assignment. One by one the children proudly read one or two pages.

The middle

The teacher asks the final child to read her story and quickly adds that she knows the child has written eight pages but there's only time for her to read out the first two pages. The child is confused and upset and dives under her desk.

The end

I reveal that I am the child and I could not have known that moment was the start of something amazing in my life. I did not know then that I would grow up with a life-long passion for communication which would influence every job I have done. With a clear communication theme established I then describe a few significant jobs or roles I've done and weave them into the theme. It's a much more memorable and creative way of communicating biographical information.[17]

Of course, not all stories have to be personal. They can give insights into the content of a presentation. For example, if you are reviewing a project, describing specific events from the project can be useful and engaging. You could describe a turning point in a project, an outstanding contribution, a dramatic moment, a sad moment, a funny moment. You get the idea.

A great word to use to start stories is the word *imagine*. It gets the brain all fired up waiting for what's next. Parables or stories from religious sources can also be used effectively in business presentations.

There's more discussion of storytelling and an exciting example in Chapter 13, 'Pitfalls and solutions' on page 160.

If you want to see a really good example of storytelling in action, take a look at a TEDx talk by Andrea Gibbs. Her topic is the power of storytelling and she walks her talk: www.youtube.com/watch?v=sh1-9xMZIfQ

Summary

If you involve an audience in a presentation you will maintain their attention and create opportunities for influence. This means:

- Good eye contact which can be improved with mind maps

- Grouping ideas around seven key points to avoid overload
- A clear structure with well-ordered ideas
- Using stories to connect to your audience
- Using stories to connect an audience to your ideas.

Reflective questions

- How comfortable are you with eye contact when speaking?
- How effective is your eye contact when presenting? How do you know?
- How likely are you to try mind maps as speaker notes?
- How can you annotate mind maps to help your delivery?
- Are you overloading your audience with information?
- Do you have more than the Magic 7 key points?
- Does the pyramid structure appeal as a preparation tool?
- Are your ideas grouped in the best order?
- What stories could be useful for your presentations?
- What function do you want your stories to perform?

Chapter 4

BE BOLD

THIS IS THE fourth of five chapters on making the most of your message. I've created a tool called BRIBE to communicate clear and compelling ideas. BRIBE is an easy-to-remember acronym with each letter representing a topic on presentation content. The acronym is explained below.

BRIBE model

B = Begin Powerfully
R = Reinforce Ideas
I = Involve the Audience
B = Be Bold
E = End Powerfully

Preview

Too many executive presentations are in the 'good enough' category. They do the job in a safe way. Somehow the speaker is not fully present, the audience are underwhelmed and the presentation is not particularly memorable.

Then out of the blue you'll get a speaker you just can't forget. Not a perfect speaker but one who is truly present; the audience is immersed in a well-prepared presentation; result – an inspired audience and an opportunity realised.

Why aren't more presentations in this second category? There's a considerable cost to an executive presentation. There's the time spent on preparation and delivery by the speaker; there's the time taken by the audience in attendance. There's time spent on event logistics. It's significant.

This chapter is about taking presentations way beyond the 'good enough' category. Ultimately, being bold is about being your best self in a presentation: authentic and fully present. Being bold is about investing the time to make your presentation fresh, interesting and engaging. Being bold is about doing presentations that make organisations better.

I am going to focus on quick and simple ways to be bold. They are:

- Being yourself
- Personal stories
- Great graphics
- Acronyms

Being yourself

The starting point for being bold in a presentation is you. Being yourself in a presentation is probably one of the boldest things you can do and few people manage it.

To be bold requires you to show up authentically and wholeheartedly. That might not happen because of nerves or a sense of not being good enough, what Brené Brown calls the culture of scarcity. The solution lies in self-acceptance and self-awareness. I believe audiences can tell when a speaker has these qualities. These speakers have a presence that suggests a presentation will be authentic and exciting.

For most of us it is a life-long journey to become more self-accepting and self-aware. As this section of the book is about content, I will stop the conversation on being yourself. However, if you want to continue this theme go to the third section of the book. It looks at our minds and how our thinking about ourselves and others can improve presentations. See page 127.

Personal stories

I am often asked for advice on how to be funny in presentations. When answering, I always acknowledge the power of humour. It can instantly transform the relationship of speaker and audience. The sharing of something funny binds two parties positively: they relax more and open up to each other. However, I usually caution against 'trying to be funny' unless you are skilled or naturally funny.

Instead, I encourage speakers to tell a personal story to bring light touches to their presentations. It can be a story of you getting things muddled. It can be a story which shows you don't take yourself too seriously. It can be a self-deprecating story. It can be amusing. It will be original material because it's from your life and not many people will have heard it. It will also provide insight about you to an audience.

Provided you speak confidently, the light touches will leap out of the story and straight into the hearts and minds of the audience. Light touches will give you the benefit of humour: a relaxed and deeper connection between you and your audience.

When I look into my own life, a few episodes in my childhood stand out. One of them was at school sports day in primary school. It was a really special day because my mum was there. She was a nurse and wasn't able to attend many school events. I watched her in the crowd as I walked to the starting line for the final of the 100m race. When the whistle blew I ran my heart out for my mother.

I started well and was in the lead. As we neared the finishing line a girl appeared, seemingly from nowhere. I willed my tired legs to maintain the narrow lead but it wasn't to be. I was overtaken and came second. It was then I started crying uncontrollably. Howling. I felt I had failed. Not even my mother could console me.

Can you believe I thought a silver medal was failure? I know, you can see right there a child with future problems that will need working out. That fiercely competitive spirit and inability to recognise achievements has played out throughout my life and been the source of success and setbacks.

This story does give a sense of who I am as a person: my vulnerabilities and strengths. If this story was introduced appropriately in a presentation, I believe you would notice my openness and feel more connected to me.

The topic of storytelling pops up throughout this book because it is fundamental to good business communication. There's another look at effective storytelling in Chapter 13 on 'Pitfalls and solutions'; see page 160.

Great graphics

I love graphics. That's why I have always enjoyed collaborating with graphic designers creating artwork for television news bulletins. Under pressure they come up with wonderful visuals. In my mind they have one of the best jobs in the newsroom.

Computer graphics in business presentations started with PowerPoint in the 1990s. Today there's more choice with the likes of Keynote and Prezi and others. I find it's relatively easy to create slides with TV-like animations using Prezi.

It is worth making slide decks look good, as research indicates that graphics can dramatically increase the retention rate of audiences.[18] Here are a few principles for making graphics work well for your audience:

- Relate to your graphics – love them!
- Less data is more
- Avoid split focus
- Use large fonts for important numbers
- Include faces of people

- Use high-contrast colours.

The following case study illustrates these ideas.

Case study

To follow this case study, you will first need to view a video of the late Swedish Professor, Hans Rosling, called '200 countries, 200 years, 4 minutes - The Joy of Stats'. It's an engaging, short video in which he describes developments in international health with the help of a BBC graphics crew. See the video in the following link: www.youtube.com/watch?v=jbkSRLYSojo. The first thing Hans Rosling demonstrates so well is the relationship between the speaker, content and graphics. He loves his graphics as much as he loves telling us about the progress of human health over two hundred years. His passion is communicated through his voice, gestures, smiles and humour. It makes him impossibly engaging!

I encourage speakers to use only graphics they love to communicate business messages with passion. It makes sense to take as much time as you reasonably can to create graphics that will powerfully serve you, your message and your audience.

Another technique Rosling does well is teasing his slides. That means he signals to his audience that a particularly important or interesting slide is coming next. When he says intensely 'look at what's about to happen!' it primes our interest and attention.

While it is clear that Professor Rosling spent significant time (and resources) developing his graphics, it is evident that his message and organisation of ideas came first. The four-minute video is the result of many, many hours of research and preparation. If you don't already know it, slides can be dangerously beguiling and take up a lot of time if you let them. To control temptation, remember that slides should always be the support act. The speaker is the main attraction for an audience.

There is a minimalist feel to the graphics in this case study even though they convey a lot of information. Rosling sticks to the principle of 'less is more' in the way he uses his graphics. Fewer images and words on a slide usually translates into more attention on the speaker and increased audience understanding of the content.

You do need to listen to what Rosling is saying to really understand the graphics. This skilfully keeps the audience's primary attention on the speaker and secondary attention on the graphics.

Rosling avoids the very common mistake of 'split focus'. This is when an audience is presented with a busy, detailed slide and the speaker keeps talking. This results in the audience being inundated with a lot of information and no opportunity to process it. So what happens? The attention of the audience is split between the speaker and the slide. The overload usually means the audience switch off to what the speaker is saying to concentrate on making sense of the slide.

Rosling's use of graphics is effective in other ways. Interesting studies are exploring the relationship between eye movements and data design.[19] The conclusions confirm that three things capture the attention of an audience quickly on a slide: high-contrasting colours, large numbers and pictures of a human face.

Rosling uses high-contrasting primary colours on his slides. There is a simple visual grammar in the use of specific colours to denote different regions of the world. The countries of Africa are represented by different-sized vivid blue circles and the countries of Asia by bright-red circles.

He also uses numbers in large fonts. The dates of his historical journey from 1810 to 2009 are animated in a large white typeface against a darker background. The data is clear, easy to follow and attractive.

The third point in the eye movement study is about the positive impact of slides featuring a human face. Rosling's graphics don't contain faces but we get to see plenty of his own highly expressive face throughout the video.

It is well worth considering how to incorporate a human face/faces when designing business slides. Organisation charts lend themselves to this quite easily. When quoting data it is also relatively easy to include a picture of the person who has provided the quote or data. But that's just the beginning – there are so many other ways to create powerful slides with pictures of people or faces!

You can be bold with photos. In avoiding obvious choices, you can end up with stunning photos that communicate meaning, evoke emotion and create impact. There's a really good blog on creating high-impact graphics by a graphics designer with the TED organisation. His photo selections are inspiring.[20]

Documentary-style slides

I saw a really bold example of slides at a book reading by Peter Snow and Ann MacMillan. Both are accomplished television anchors in the UK and Canada and they did a presentation on their book *War Stories* in the style of a television documentary. They used well over 100 slides in their 30-minute fast-paced, high-energy presentation. The content did lend itself to that style in the way it told stories of individual war heroes with lots of photos and pictures of people, places, action and landscapes. It felt like voiceovers in a live documentary although obviously we could see them on stage. It would be exciting to see that format translated into an executive presentation.

Acronyms

These are quick, easy ways to remember ideas. I have been using BRIBE for years to help participants remember my content model. It is effective because it brings together a wide range of ideas in an easy-to-remember format. Sometimes I support the acronym with an image, sometimes not. 'BRIBE' typically brings to mind images of brown envelopes or stacks of cash! At different times I have used both of these images when explaining BRIBE.

Acronyms give speakers the opportunity to be creative and memorable with their messaging.

Let's work with an example. Take the letters 'BBC' – familiar to many people as standing for The British Broadcasting Corporation and representing a long-established global media brand. Using the acronym technique I can create an executive presentation using the same three letters but they would stand for something entirely different.

If I was doing a short presentation on how to begin a speech powerfully, I could structure my content around the BBC acronym denoting the following three points:

B – Body

B – Breath

C – Creativity.

So, my presentation on how to begin a presentation powerfully could work something like this:

Element of the presentation	Letter of acronym	Description of content
Intro	-	This presentation shows you the 'BBC' model to start a speech with impact.

Key point 1	B – Body	How you use your body has an impact on your audience even before you start speaking. Focus on facial expression, gestures, posture, physical energy to give your presentation a strong start.
Key point 2	B – Breath	Breath. This section discusses diaphragmatic breath and how important it is for high-grade public speaking. I explain how to breathe with the diaphragm.
Key point 3	C – Creativity	Encourage speakers to lose their reluctance to be creative in executive presentations. Show compelling examples. The use of the acronym BBC in the presentation is itself a creative device.
Outro	-	Concluding remarks.

Figure 5: BBC acronym

The BBC acronym has a useful structural function. It provides a simple flow of ideas. A clear, effective structure is often a hallmark of a successful presentation.

The acronym provides another benefit. The letters BBC will be strongly linked to the media. If I was actually giving this presentation I could use this association to reinforce my own media credentials as a former BBC news anchor. With the entire structure of the presentation developed around the letters 'BBC', it would be virtually impossible for an audience to forget my media credentials and connections.

Acronyms can relate closely to themes as in the BBC example above. Alternatively they can be unrelated like the BRIBE acronym. Either way, they are good tools for making presentations bold.

Summary

The boldest thing you can do in a presentation is be yourself. Your best self. Personal stories will enrich presentations and give them unique content. Graphics are an easy way to go bold. Love them, and use bright colours, large fonts and faces. Acronyms are a simple device that work well in presentations.

Reflective questions

- How close are you to being yourself in presentations?
- Are there any barriers?
- How can you address them?
- What childhood stories can you use in presentations?
- What personal stories reveal your strengths and vulnerabilities?
- Do you have amusing stories about yourself to use in a presentation?
- Do you love your graphics?
- If not, what do you need to do to change that?
- How much time will you allow for creating good visuals?
- Do your slides have consistent visual grammar?
- What makes a photo high impact?
- Are acronyms for you?
- What interesting acronyms can you come up with?

Chapter 5

END POWERFULLY

THIS IS THE last of five chapters on making the most of your message. I've created a tool called BRIBE to communicate clear and compelling ideas. BRIBE is an easy-to-remember acronym with each letter representing a topic on presentation content. The acronym is explained below.

BRIBE model

B = Begin Powerfully
R = Reinforce Ideas
I = Involve the Audience
B = Be Bold
E = End Powerfully

Preview

The end of a presentation can be a fascinating place: speakers do all manner of things. Some embark on a verbal sprint to the finishing line; some visibly relax because they know it's nearly over; some continue to cling to the podium for dear life, semi-paralysed; some deliver the best bit; some have razzmatazz endings with props, videos and music; some just quietly fizzle out and others come to an abrupt stop. Clearly some of these endings work better than others.

With so many ways to do an effective ending, the most useful thing I can do here is emphasise the must-do things that apply to virtually all presentations. They are:

- The Flag – lets the audience know the presentation is about to end
- The Review – recaps key ideas from the speech
- The Call – lets the audience know what action they need to take
- The Out – the device that actually ends the presentation

Before I explain these points I want to emphasise why the end needs so much attention. It's when the audience is highly attentive and what you say in the closing moments is most likely to be remembered. Psychologists call it the *Recency Effect*.

And it's something we've known about for quite a while – as long ago as 1885! That's when memory studies done by German psychologist Hermann Ebbinghaus described the serial position effect. He observed that the ability to remember items in a list depended on their position in the list. Items at the beginning and end were more memorable than those in the middle. And people recall items at the end before those at the beginning.[21]

I see a similar effect with presentations when I talk to delegates after a speech. It's very likely audiences will remember what you say at the end so make it count. *The Flag* is one way to do this.

The Flag

To make the most of the recency effect let audiences know the end is coming. One way to do this is to signal the end. It can be done successfully with a slide but most people choose to do it with simple phrases. For example:

- 'To conclude my presentation'
- 'And finally'
- 'The last thing I want to say is…'
- 'To end, I'd like to leave you with…'

Don't underestimate the power of these phrases. Audiences react quite noticeably to them. There's often a shift in body position – people sit up more attentively or look up with interested eyes. The energy level in the room surges. It's a good time to re-state important ideas or key messages.

But there is a caveat: end must mean end.

I say this because I once attended a presentation where the speaker repeatedly flagged the end of his presentation. I think there were five or six Flags. Each one sorely tested the patience of the audience. You could see them start to flinch each time he said 'and finally'. By the time he did make it to the end the air was thick with frustration. Be warned!

The Review and the Call

There are so many ways to review your presentation or summarise what you've said including bullet points, mind maps, a graphic, a story or a quote. Make sure you keep the *Review* clear and sharp and think about whether you want to summarise a single global point or a few key messages.

The *Call* is sometimes called the *Call to Action*. It lets the audience know exactly what you want them to do next. It's the purpose of the presentation so express the Call clearly and explicitly.

The Out

The *Out* is something special. It models the 'and finally' story in a news bulletin. In TV its purpose is to leave the audience with something uplifting after hard news items. In business an 'out' can have a similar uplifting function.

The Out is the last thing an audience hears or sees: a question, a new thought, a new graphic, a plea, a gesture. All of these can be good 'outs'.

One I particularly like is an 'out' that references a point made at the beginning of a presentation. I call it top'n'tailing. It combines the benefit of the primacy and recency effect so it usually works well. It can be something as simple as recalling an image, quote or item of data that started the presentation. Let's say, for example, you start an executive presentation with a striking quote from a leading economist. When you return to that quote at the end of your speech, it triggers an almost involuntary act on the part of the audience to think about what you said at the beginning and also the intervening points.

Case study: Kanye West

I have an intriguing example of an 'out' below. It's from international rap artist, Kanye West, and I appreciate it is not an obviously corporate example. It is though a great illustration of making the most of the end of a speech.

It happened at the 47th Grammy Awards ceremony. Kanye West comes up to the podium to accept the award for best Rap Album and in two minutes gives a masterclass in public speaking. Go to the following link to view the video clip: www.grammy.com/grammys/videos/2005-grammys-kanye-west-wins-best-rap-album

1. Kanye West cuts a commanding presence from the beginning and lets the audience know that he's going to take his time to speak. His tone and body language indicate he has something important to say. There are measures of intensity and vulnerability.

2. West says 'nothing in life is promised except death'. He is using a quote usually attributed to American writer and politician, Benjamin Franklin. In 1789 Franklin wrote that 'nothing in life is certain except death and taxes'.

West has clearly spent some time preparing this speech. The quote instantly elevates his speech above the standard of most acceptance speeches. The quote signals the serious tone of the speech. It also signals the theme of the speech, which is appreciating every moment in life.

3. The reflective tone gives way to excitement and energy as West celebrates his moment. He tell us he is going to scream and shout and pop champagne as he accepts his Grammy. The fizzing energy of this section of the speech contrasts with the beginning.

4. Then West starts the end of his speech with a question. Returning to his quieter, more reflective tone, he says 'what everyone wants to know is what I would do if I DIDN'T win the award?' He is clearly referencing his bad boy reputation and teasing his audience.

5. We then get a 'power pause' (extended pause) that creates suspense and allows curiosity to ferment. He then delivers his punch line, 'I guess we'll never know!' and there's much laughing and thunderous applause.

There is a great lesson here for executives to learn about control and timing; about pausing and making even the last seconds count.

Summary

Give thought to the end of a presentation. Be clear about what you want your audience to remember and the best way to do that.

- Let audiences know that you are concluding your speech with a Flag.

- Remind the audience of the theme or key points when you review.
- Be explicit when you state the Call so the audience know exactly what action they need to take.
- Come up with an 'out' that is right for your personality, your presentation and your audience.

Reflective questions

- What effective Flags have you seen speakers use?
- How do you usually flag the end of your presentation?
- What other Flags might work for you?
- Will you use different Flags for different types of presentations?
- How could you make a visual Flag work?
- What points need to be in your review?
- What tone suits the review?
- Where will you get ideas for good 'outs'?
- Will you use the top'n'tail 'out'?

Chapter 6

WHEN JACQUI MET HARRY OR USING SCRIPTS

Figure 6: Prince Harry with Jacqui Harper, July 2017

Photographer David Cole: © Leeds Community Foundation

I'VE SPOKEN AT more than 300 conferences yet when asked to speak to royalty I was *so* nervous! I sorted my nerves by writing a professional script. It worked. The conference organiser described my presentation as 'assured, business-like and warm'.

Preview

I don't often use scripts when speaking but sometimes it's the best option. In this chapter I share techniques to speak well with scripts. They are:

- Rewrite
- Rehearse
- Mark up scripts
- Fine-tune
- What to do on the day
- Using smartphones and tablets

Rewrite

The goal is to get the script to sound as close as possible to your speaking voice. The success of the presentation is down to how effectively you write or rewrite the script to sound 'natural'.

The conference organisers wrote a script for me to introduce the conference, the guests and to close the conference. The content of the script was excellent but the language didn't sound like me. My first task was to transform the script into 'Jacqui speak'.

As I sat at my laptop going through the script I was constantly reading the words out loud to hear how the language sounded and testing whether it felt like something I would actually say. This is a practice I learned in TV newsrooms.

I shortened the sentences so they were easier to say and therefore easier to communicate the meaning.

I changed words so the tone was more conversational. For example, after showing a video clip of young people talking about mental health I had to say a back anno (TV speak for a back announcement, that is, a short comment after a video).

The original script said:

Thank you to these incredible people, who are here today, for sharing their very personal stories.

The rewritten script:

Such incredible young people. Thank you for sharing your stories. And it's great to have you here today.

I used contracted versions of familiar phrases; for example, 'I have' was changed to 'I've' and 'we are' was changed to 'we're'.

I used 'set up' phrases to introduce important ideas before actually saying them. For example, there was data on mental health that I wanted the audience to really notice. I prefaced the data by saying 'I'd like to share a couple of important stats with you'. It helps to prime the audience to pay particular attention.

Double line spacing makes a script so much easier to navigate in a live situation. It means when looking up and down from the script it is easy to find your place and keep regular eye contact with the audience.

I have occasionally seen speakers falter (and worse) when their script pages come out of order. One solution is to staple the script pages or link them together with a treasury tag. The only drawback to these options is that a sensitive mike will pick up the sound of the pages being turned and the script will also be more visible to the audience.

Another option is to number the script pages. I am talking numbers written in big, black felt tip pen so in the event of pages becoming disordered it is super easy to get everything back in the right order. Once numbered, hold the pages together with a paper clip. At the podium remove the paper clip so you can slide the pages from right to left as you are reading. This keeps the paper-shuffling sound to a minimum and is less visible to the audience. This is how I've handled scripts when broadcasting live on television.

Rehearse

Once I got the script sounding right I moved onto rehearsals. In my office I stood up to read scripts all the way through – several times. The point was to become comfortably familiar with the script but not to the point of knowing it by heart.

Mark up scripts

After several run-throughs I returned to my desk and the script. This time my goal was to use annotations to enhance my presence and impact. There are many ways to do this and I encourage you to create a system that works for you. My system included underlining words that needed vocal emphasis. I inserted an asterisk where I wanted to remind myself to pause within a paragraph.

I circled an asterisk to prompt me to do a 'power pause'. This is a longer pause that separates one key idea from another. It allows the speaker to breathe and the audience to process the information, and it signals to the audience that a new, key idea is about to start.

I highlighted in yellow the names of the sponsors so their name checks were given sufficient vocal weight.

See Figure 7 for the first page of my conference script and the markup I did.

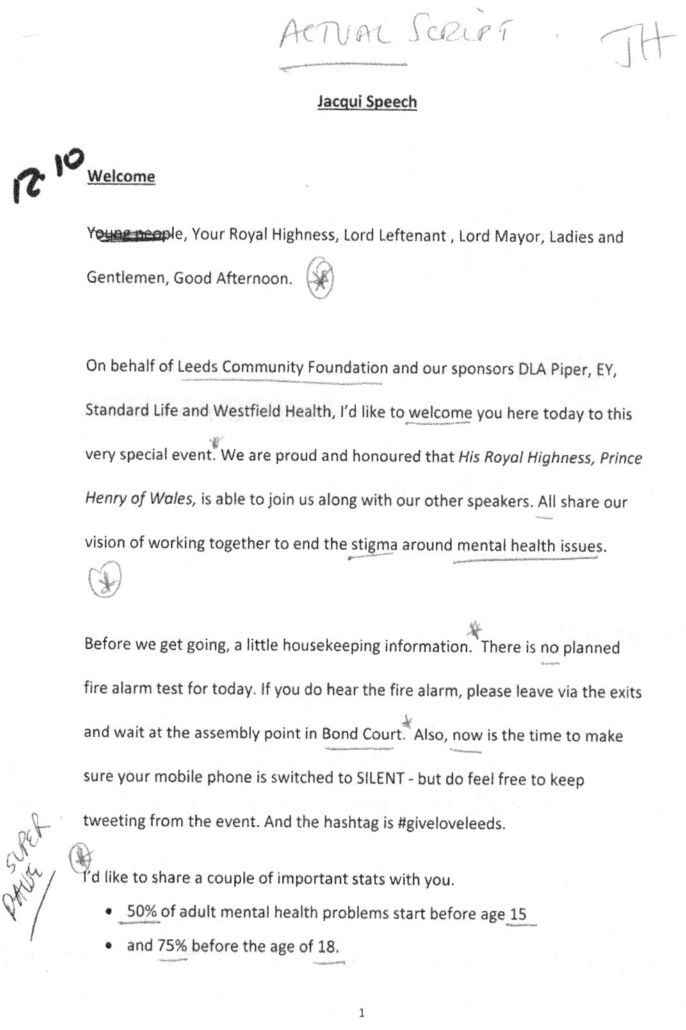

ACTUAL SCRIPT . JH

Jacqui Speech

R. 10 <u>Welcome</u>

~~Young people~~, Your Royal Highness, Lord Leftenant , Lord Mayor, Ladies and Gentlemen, Good Afternoon.

On behalf of Leeds Community Foundation and our sponsors DLA Piper, EY, Standard Life and Westfield Health, I'd like to welcome you here today to this very special event. We are proud and honoured that *His Royal Highness, Prince Henry of Wales*, is able to join us along with our other speakers. All share our vision of working together to end the stigma around mental health issues.

Before we get going, a little housekeeping information. There is no planned fire alarm test for today. If you do hear the fire alarm, please leave via the exits and wait at the assembly point in Bond Court. Also, now is the time to make sure your mobile phone is switched to SILENT - but do feel free to keep tweeting from the event. And the hashtag is #giveloveleeds.

SUPER DRIVE I'd like to share a couple of important stats with you.

- 50% of adult mental health problems start before age 15
- and 75% before the age of 18.

1

Figure 7: Jacqui script with markups

Fine-tune

Then it was back to rehearsals to fine-tune my performance. This time I recorded the rehearsals to see what needed adjusting. For the first rehearsal I had the camera lens covered so I recorded sound only. This helped to assess how fluently I came across and to gauge the expressiveness in my voice.

The second run-through I just watched vision and muted the sound. I was checking my body language, gestures, facial animation etc.

In the last rehearsal I reviewed both sound and vision. By this time I was very happy and comfortable with the script.

I was able to do a full walk-through at the venue the day before. I used the opportunity to 'own the space'. This is a combination of breathing into the space, testing mikes and walking to and from the podium.

On the day!

In the early morning I read through the scripts in private. On the day of an event it's amazing how the adrenaline suddenly kicks in and makes you feel as if you haven't done any preparation at all. The solution is to focus on the start of the speech.

This is when the audience is most attentive and when the rapport between speaker and audience is established. It's also when a speaker is most likely to be nervous. For this reason I recommend going over the beginning of the script as many times as you need. I went through my opening *five* times in private!

With all that preparation behind me I was finally ready for the Prince!

Smartphones and tablets

A quick word about smartphones and tablets. I have seen people speak effectively from scripts on their smartphones or tablets. I am not a huge fan but that might be me being old school (also I never truly trust technology; it has let me down too often).

I can definitely see electronic devices working well as speaker prompts in less formal meetings. You can mark up the script using the ink feature in your word processing software.

It's also a good idea to make sure the power option on your device is set to 'always on'. This avoids your script disappearing from the screen when you're in the middle of speaking.

Summary

- Rewrite the script to achieve your natural speaking voice
- Rehearse just enough to become familiar with the content
- Mark up scripts for emphasis, clarity and impact
- Print a backup script in case of problems on the day
- Fine-tune to achieve a strong, positive presence
- On the day, focus on the opening words. Get them right
- When using smartphones or tablets, disable the auto standby feature.

Reflective questions

- How well does your script reflect your natural speaking voice?
- Is the script layout easy to read in a live situation?
- How will you keep your pages in order?

- Can you cope easily if your script falls onto the floor and pages become disordered?
- Do you recognise when you are comfortably familiar with a script?
- What's your script markup system?
- What are your recorded rehearsals telling you?
- What technique helps you stay in control at the beginning?

Chapter 7

VOCAL PRESENCE

Preview

THIS CHAPTER IS about developing vocal presence to improve executive presentations. It covers:

- What vocal presence is and why it matters
- How to do a Presence Audit for authentic speech
- Vocal competence exercises: diaphragm breathing
- Vocal competence exercises: improving the sound of the voice
- Vocal competence exercises: fine-tuning the voice

Why vocal presence matters

Research done in 2014 illustrated the need for strong vocal presence from the very first utterance in a presentation. This was concluded after looking at judgements of personality made by individuals listening to over 300 unknown voices for the first time. After hearing just the word 'Hello', listeners decided on the speaker's personality. The personality traits they selected from included:

Aggressiveness

Attractiveness

Competence

Confidence

Dominance

Femininity

Likeability

Masculinity

Trustworthiness

Warmth.

The findings showed that different listeners tended to have similar perceptions of particular voices. Researchers concluded that the initial impression formed from hearing less than a second of sound of someone's voice was likely to be the same impression held after listening to the voice for a longer period.

The research also revealed that perceptions of trust and likeability were connected to speech with varied pitch. Furthermore, hearing an attractive voice increased how much listeners perceived qualities of trust and likeability. In males vocal attractiveness was to do with perceptions of strength while in females vocal attractiveness was about sensing warmth and trustworthiness.[22]

Improving vocal presence helps achieve vocal attractiveness, varied pitch and the all-important trust. Strong vocal presence is critical in naked presentations where an executive is not using any supporting visuals. It's also particularly important in audio conferences, phone meetings and webinars when the speaker is not seen by the participants.

Strong vocal presence is the alignment of who we are and the intentional way we use voice to express ideas. The first step in developing vocal presence is conducting a Presence Audit.

The Presence Audit

The Presence Audit describes who you want to be as a human being. It is the foundation for more authentic expression of the voice as it guides voice development. I use the word *audit* here because this activity is about data collection and evaluation for the purpose of future improvement – much like any other audit.

The Presence Audit has two stages:

1. Collect and evaluate data about presence

2. Create a three-word report to drive your future improvement.

Presence Audit: Collect and evaluate data

It's time to reflect on your presentations and here are some questions to ask yourself:

- Which have been my best presentations and why?
- Which presentations didn't go so well and why?
- How would I describe my presence in both cases above?
- How would I describe my presence today?

What answers would colleagues, friends and loved ones give to the questions above? Brainstorm and write down the answers. The data will be even richer if you actually ask people for their feedback on your presence.

The information gives a useful picture of how you are currently coming across in presentations. Now reduce the comments to single words.

But what if you stand in 'the place of possibility'?[23] If you stand in a place where you can see your future self excelling in so many ways when presenting, what words would capture that excellence? What words would describe your presence? Does your existing list contain the words or do you need to add words?

Presence Audit: Three-word report

The goal is to select three words from the data you've collected to capture the presence of the future, brilliant you.

Why three words you ask? A fellow executive coach, Heidi Swartz, sent me an article about dumping long-winded New Year resolutions and replacing them with a single word. It got my attention. The idea is that one word filters decisions better, increases focus, is practical and easy to remember. It's not so easily 'broken' like a resolution or written statement. This in turn increases the prospects of making and maintaining the change.[24]

I instinctively felt that one word was too reductive for the purpose of the Presence Audit. Three words offer more nuance and seem more useful. That's why I have settled on the power of three words.

So when you look at the words in your data collection, which seem most useful for you going forward as an executive presenter? Underline them.

Now take a long, hard look at the words underlined and settle on three words.

Write them down. These words are like gold dust because they can help you lean into your future. Put them on your desktop, smartphone or fridge. Maybe even make them your new password! See them several times every day. High visibility will help embed them in your life and in your vocal presence.

An item from my data collection:

> When I did this reflection exercise for myself, up popped a memory I had long chosen to forget. It's under the category of presentations that didn't go so well.
>
> Years ago I accepted an invitation to speak at a conference on a topic that wasn't really my area of expertise. I knew as soon as I accepted the invitation

it was a mistake. I told myself that if I did thorough research and preparation, my presentation skills were strong enough to wing it.

No way. The audience saw right through me. It was a miserable experience for me and my audience.

Although the audience will have got something from my presentation, they could have got a whole lot more if I had been speaking on my specialist topics.

Evaluation: my presence throughout this presentation was inauthentic, superficial and uncomfortable.

My desired presence going forward from this episode is to be authentic, thoughtful and relaxed.

Jacqui's Presence Audit

I was given a Presence Audit (inadvertently) by a client. I mentioned in Chapter 6, on using scripts, that I hosted a conference in the city of Leeds in the UK and my client wrote a note to thank me and described my presence as 'assured, business-like and warm'. I was pleased with these words. Assured and business-like were important qualities for the high-powered business audience I was addressing.

But I was particularly happy to see she included the word 'warm'. It indicated that I had made a personal connection to the audience of over 300 people. I have brainstormed many words for my Presence Audit and I find that I am really happy to use the ones generated by my client. Because I am picky with words I have used synonyms for assured and business-like. I have replaced assured with confident and business-like with professional so the Presence Audit for my future improvement is:

- *Confident*
- *Professional*
- *Warm.*

The Presence Audit is a tool for building self-awareness and self-development. It provides a clear outcome for the changes you might consider making to your voice. For more information on techniques and strategies to develop presence by the way we think, see page 127 in the third section of the book on the mind.

Vocal competence

The Presence Audit gives us the foundation and framework for vocal competence. The areas of competence we look at are diaphragm breathing, resonance and fine-tuning the voice.

The voice is wonderfully unique. No one else in the world sounds exactly the same (maybe with the exception of some twins). Yet it's remarkable that such a vital part of our identity and professional toolkit should be so underdeveloped. Too many executives think the voice is something fixed rather than something that can be developed.

The human voice has no system of its own – instead it uses parts of the respiratory system and the digestive system. So when we are improving the voice, some of the activity is connected to the respiratory system, for example diaphragm breathing. Some activity is to do with the digestive system, like articulation exercises using the lips, mouth and teeth.

The rest of this chapter provides easy activities to achieve vocal competence. We start with the cornerstone of vocal competence, diaphragm breathing.

Vocal competence: Diaphragm breathing

Some of the most vocally competent speakers I have come across in my work as a communication coach have been leaders from a military background. I believe it's their high level of fitness that results in the effectiveness of their diaphragm muscle driving air out of the lungs. It makes their voices sound so magnificent: powerful, clear and energetic.

To use the diaphragm effectively takes time and practice. Breathing with the diaphragm is actually something we do automatically as newborn babies. Then over the years poor breathing habits start and eventually become established. This is why diaphragm breathing sometimes feels counter-intuitive for adults. Many people I work with do shallow chest breathing and have huge potential to improve their vocal power.

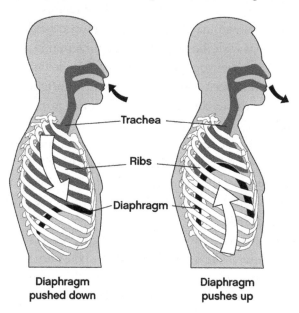

Diaphragm
pushed down

Diaphragm
pushes up

Figure 8: Diaphragm breathing

It can be quite straightforward to practise diaphragm breathing once you know the mechanics of breath. Figure 8 shows the diaphragm muscle located just underneath the lungs.

The image on the left-hand side of Figure 8 shows what happens when we breathe in air: the lungs expand and the diaphragm gets pushed down to allow the intake of as much air as possible.

Then when we breathe out, the diaphragm pushes the air upwards as the lungs get smaller and air comes out of the mouth as indicated in the image on the right-hand side of Figure 8.

The easiest way to practise diaphragm breathing is to lie on the floor and put your hands gently on your abdomen. Breathe in to the count of three and notice your abdomen rise. You've got it right when you breathe in and at the same time your stomach moves out. Now exhale over three counts. When you breathe out, your stomach should move inward forcing the air out of the lungs with the help of the diaphragm muscle.

Once you know you have this right lying down, it's useful to stand up and check your technique when upright or sitting on a chair as many presentations are done seated around a board table.

So, standing or seated, put your hands around the sides of your ribcage. Breathe in deeply so your hands are pushed outwards. Release the breath. Make sure that you are not lifting your shoulders up and if they become tense give them a shrug and a shake.

Now put your hands around your waist, breathe in and as you breathe out make a 'shhh' sound. As you breathe out feel the muscles around your waist and stomach moving inwards as they support the air out of your body.

When you are ready to progress, take in enough breath so you can breathe out on a count of five or more. To really activate the power of diaphragm breathing, practise increasing the out breath to at least 20 counts over two weeks.

Vocal competence: Resonance

Resonance is the amplification of sound in our chest, throat and head. Paying attention to our three resonating chambers with regular exercises will give the voice a richer sound that many people associate with gravitas.

When teaching I make quite a fuss about the vocal cords (see Figure 9) because it is the jewel in the vocal crown. The vocal cords are located in the throat and consist of two folds which vibrate and elongate to produce sound. You can feel the folds vibrating if you gently hold your neck with one hand and hum. If you hum a high note the reverberation is less noticeable. If you go for a deeper note you can feel a longer elongation of the cord.

There are many ways to warm up the vocal cords. My favourite is humming a tune because it's easy, effective and quick.

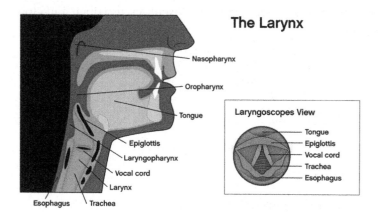

Figure 9: Vocal cords

We now move from the throat to the head resonators: the tongue, lips and teeth, and soft palate.

The tongue plays a significant role in how the voice sounds. It is a strong muscular organ with a big digestive function of swallowing and pushing food around as we chew. For speech it functions best when relaxed at the root. These exercises will help reduce root tension. Try the following tongue movements.

Move your tongue out and in then up, to the side, down and then to the other side.

Now say out loud the following sounds. You will notice that they really get the tongue working.

Ta Ta Ta Ta

La La La La

Na Na Na Na

Lily, Lily, Lily, Lily

Tell Terry Tucker and Tommy Tatler not to tell tales

Now the lips. The following exercises encourage the lips to move positions efficiently. The exercises also open and close the lips.

Say the following out loud:

Eee, Ooo, Eee, Ooo

Ma Ma Ma Ma

Pa Pa Pa Pa

Ba Ba Ba Ba

Mwa Mwa Mwa Mwa

Sweet Sue, Sweet Sue

Now it's the turn of the soft palate. It's at the back of the roof of the mouth and consists of muscle and connective tissue. It helps to make most of the sounds of speech. A soft palate that is not working optimally makes speech sound nasal and weak.

You can wake up the soft palate with a simple yawn. How hard is that?

Another exercise for the soft palate involves making sounds. Say the following out loud:

Ka Ka Ka Ka

Ga Ga Ga Ga

Nga Nga Nga Nga

Kick Cake and Coke Quite Quickly

Vocal competence: Fine-tuning

Now that we've got major muscles and resonators working, it's time to start fine-tuning and work with words. Tongue twisters are fantastic for speaking with clarity and precision. They are particularly helpful for executives speaking in a second language or addressing international audiences.

Tongue twisters

Say with as much clarity, passion and purpose as you can!

Red lorry, yellow lorry

Red leather, yellow leather

Rubber baby buggy bumpers

Now make it a little harder by saying it with the same precision but a little faster.

My executives know how fond I am of *Peter Piper the Pickled Pepper Picker*. When articulation is what we need to work on, I challenge them to make Peter Piper the most urgent business news of the day. Watching a roomful of ambitious, international executives commit to this exercise always makes me feel joyful. I share it with you because it is such an effective tool: it makes your jaw, lips, tongue and teeth work hard and subsequently speech sounds clearer and sharper. Enjoy.

Peter Piper the pickled pepper picker,

picked a peck of pickled pepper.

If Peter Piper picked a peck of pickled pepper

where's the peck of pickled pepper

that Peter Piper the pickled pepper picker picked?

Often the articulation of Peter Piper can be improved with hand gestures and facial expressions. I don't prescribe gestures as I prefer participants to discover and use the particular gestures that work best for them.

If you'd like some more tongue twisters, there are some excellent, challenging international tongue twisters at the following website: www.lexiophiles.com/uncategorized/ practice-your-pronunciation

Placing meaning

Ensuring audiences understand the meaning and focus of our presentations is central to successful communication. I encourage students to emphasise particular words.

When teaching I get participants to work on poetry or dramatic speech. My INSEAD colleague Steve Knight re-introduced me to 'Invictus' by Victorian poet William Ernest Henley. I had not seen the poem since school days. Many people will associate the poem with the late President of South Africa, Nelson Mandela. He used the poem to keep his spirit alive when imprisoned on Robben Island. It's easy to see why he found the words so powerful and inspiring.

Here are two lines from the poem:

I am the master of my fate,

I am the captain of my soul.

Part 1 of the exercise on placing meaning

To do the first part of this exercise, concentrate on the first line only: 'I am the master of my fate'. Say the line out loud and each time you say the entire line emphasise a different word as underlined in the following. Don't just say the words. Express a really significant thought each time you say a line.

_I_ am the master of my fate

I _am_ the master of my fate

I am _the_ master of my fate

I am the _master_ of my fate

I am the master _of_ my fate

I am the master of _my_ fate

I am the master of my _fate_

Part 2 of the exercise on placing meaning

The second part of the exercise is done with the first line of a real presentation. Do exactly the same activity but this time use a single sentence from a business presentation. Emphasise a different word each time you say the whole sentence. It could be the opening or close of a presentation or explaining a key point.

The goal is to go into all presentations being intentional about the words you emphasise and how you shape meaning for your audience.

Power Pause

I spend a lot of time getting executives to pause more frequently when speaking. When speakers pause at the end of a sentence they achieve two things. They give the audience time to process what's been said and they also give themselves time to breathe before starting a new point.

Many executives pause for what feels like a microsecond. That's just not long enough to achieve the points identified above. A purposeful pause when speaking between sentences, or within sentences, is enough to increase the impact of what's being said. It also provides valuable thinking time for the speaker before she or he says the next point. It has the wonderful effect of helping a speaker feel in control. I call it a Power Pause.

A Power Pause has no specific time duration. A Power Pause may take longer at important junctions in a presentation, for example between key points. It's really about the time it takes to command attention. It's one of those little actions that delivers big results.

I recognise it does take courage to be silent a bit longer than you're used to and especially under the scrutiny of an audience. That's usually when people want to avoid quiet moments and instead fill every space with the sound of their voice. Initially, you may have to step outside your comfort zone to do the Power Pause but it's highly worthwhile. Start with small increments when speaking on the phone or online. Get feedback from trusted colleagues as you transform your presentations with Power Pauses.

Some executives find it helpful to write a Power Pause in their notes or scripts. I've seen some people write prompts in scripts in red ink. I've seen others use an asterisk to denote a pause and two asterisks to represent a Power Pause. Devise whatever scheme works for you.

Practising vocal competence

I have three levels of practice: gold, silver and bronze.

Gold

Gold-level practice is achieved from daily work. It can be as short as five minutes each day doing three activities.

The first and non-optional activity is taking time to focus on diaphragm breathing. Spend a couple of minutes tuning into yourself and taking deep, natural breaths.

Then choose one activity to improve the resonance of your voice and its gravitas.

I would suggest humming a simple tune like 'Happy Birthday' or your favourite song. This will gently warm up the vocal cords and prepare your voice for the work ahead.

And finally select one activity to fine-tune your voice. I would go for Power Pauses. Practise by reading business stories aloud from your smartphone. Read the sentences with purpose and passion. End each sentence with a Power Pause. Elevate the ideas with your delivery.

Silver

Silver-level practice is regular practice but with less frequency, say every few days or once a week. You do one activity from each of the three categories: breathing, resonance and fine-tuning. It's still beneficial but won't get optimal results.

Bronze

Bronze-level practice is done on an ad hoc basis. An example of this would be doing three practice activities on the day of a presentation. It will still make a difference to your vocal presence.

If you have time to record your speaking voice during vocal competence work, it presents an excellent opportunity to assess your vocal presence. Are the qualities identified in your Presence Audit showing up in your voice? If not, why not? How can you achieve a closer alignment?

One final item on how to increase the impact of vocal presence comes from voice coach Michaela Kennen. She works with clients preparing business presentations and works with actors on the West End stage in London's theatre land.

Her advice is to 'Follow the Full Stop'.

When we write language we do it in a structured way. We use paragraphs, sentences, full stops, colons and commas to separate ideas, indicate emphasis and take a breath.

When we speak, however, we don't do that. We often speak as if there was a stream of words with no paragraphs and no full stops. It's a big flow. The result is sentences that don't end properly and the speaker doesn't take a breath. Instead you snatch breath.

For a better voice, focus on ending sentences. Formulate ideas so you can use a proper downward inflexion to end sentences. Then your body can take a breath. Practise doing this at the beginning of a presentation so your body gets into the rhythm of landing an idea and taking a breath.

When I work with actors in the theatre I get them to communicate the punctuation. Punctuation gives physical signals for where to breathe.

For executives to communicate the punctuation, they need clarity on what they are saying. When the ideas are clear and succinct, speakers will take a deep, natural breath and the voice will make a downward inflexion when needed.

As a communicator you achieve impact when you understand the structure of a spoken sentence. In spoken English, the voice goes over the top of the phrase and down at the end of the sentence. This pattern helps us communicate meaning clearly. You can never really give a message impact and make it meaningful to other people without using the voice in this way.

Impact is also increased with rehearsal. In the theatre, people would think it insane for someone to stand up and speak ideas out loud for the first time without rehearsal.

Even when I am training clients I will rehearse my opening remarks. I say them out loud. Every time I say the opening it is different because the clients are different. The opening contains core ideas that are tailored to what's happening on the day.

I will practise the opening for five minutes before leaving home. I spend that time organising my thoughts and structuring the beginning.

Practising saying ideas out loud makes a big difference to impact. It creates the shift to spoken language.

Pitch notes in the voice create passion. Increasing your pitch will lead you to communicating with greater passion. It's the pitch that shows people what you mean, what you care about and what's important.

Voice and dialect expert, Michaela Kennen

Summary

This chapter has covered how to speak with an authentic and competent voice. This is vocal presence. Use it to give effective 'naked presentations' and make a strong, initial impact.

The Presence Audit guides voice development to authenticity. The Audit is a three-word report describing our ideal presence.

To achieve vocal competence there are three elements to work on: diaphragm breathing, improving resonance and fine-tuning the voice. Humming helps resonance and tongue twisters help articulation.

Reflective questions

- What do you like about your voice?
- What would you like to develop in your voice?
- How well does your voice serve you when presenting?
- Does your voice convey you at your best?
- What feedback do you get about your voice?
- Whose voice do you admire? Why?
- How effective are you at naked presentations? What do you need to work on?
- Will you practise diaphragm breathing?
- Which exercise is most useful to you for developing resonance?
- Which exercise is most useful to you for fine-tuning your voice?
- What will you include in your vocal competence work?
- Are you ready to Power Pause?

Chapter 8

BODY LANGUAGE

I

T WAS THE silent, black and white movie, *The Artist* (2011), that gave me a glorious reminder of the power of body language: how riveting a look of the eye can be, an expressive face, a small gesture or a sudden body movement.

In business communication it's hard to imagine the equivalent of a silent movie but there's no doubt that body language can be a big help in communicating ideas and important information.

Preview

This chapter explores how body language can help with the following:
- Support speaker credibility
- Increase rapport with an audience
- Increase the impact of a business message

It would be marvellous if body language was simply a matter of a specific movement causing a predictable response. The way body language works is far from precise; it has a messiness about it. This is because our bodies send conscious and unconscious signals to an audience. The audience can decode those signals in varying ways and also misinterpret what they see. This gives plenty of opportunity for things to go awry.[25]

So while it's impossible to guarantee the results of conscious body language there are still many things speakers can do to improve an executive presentation.

Body language to support speaker credibility

A presentation is a credibility exercise.[26]

I really like this description because it neatly expresses the idea that credibility is at the heart of a successful presentation. Many things will contribute to that credibility, including the perception of professionalism.

As soon as an audience sets eyes on a speaker, they are judging the personal qualities, competence and professionalism of that speaker. It's thought that the impressions formed in the first five seconds, what researchers call 'thin slices of behaviour', overwhelmingly tends to be the same view held after a much longer period, say for example, at the end of a presentation.[27]

Walk-on

With this five-second, first-impression window in mind, it is useful to focus on the way you walk to a podium to start a presentation. A brisk walk with energy, purpose and an upright posture commands attention and builds credibility. It can deliver the business equivalent of love at first sight, according to Allan and Barbara Pease.[28] Their book on body language has lots of useful ideas.

Perhaps the most stunning example of a walk-on I have seen was done by Hollywood actor Michael Douglas. He was presenting an award at the annual event for the British Academy of Film and Television. He was called onto the stage and walked on in less than four seconds. That sentence does not begin to convey the impact of his entrance. I was in the auditorium enthralled as were other Academy members.

He was impeccably dressed in a well-cut, well-fitting suit in beautiful cloth. I believe he was in black tie. His grooming was flawless. He cut such a fabulous figure as he emerged from the side of the stage. He exuded confidence, style and power. He walked to the podium with energy and poise and he didn't rush. Before he said a word the audience was gripped and excited.

Now I know that a lot of the audience reaction was down to the celebrity star power of Michael Douglas as a Hollywood A-list actor. However, I believe his ability to use physical presence so powerfully is something potentially available to all of us in the corporate world.

You certainly don't need Michael's acting skills to give a confident, highly professional impression as you walk on stage. If you think there's room for improvement in your walk-on, use rehearsal time to practise. Record yourself if at all possible. Pay attention to (PPE!) posture, pace and expression (facial).

Grounded posture

Once at the podium or in the middle of a stage I encourage speakers to adopt a grounded posture to start a presentation. It looks confident and facilitates gestures. A grounded posture means standing with your feet about hip-width apart with softly bent knees, an upright posture and hands loosely at the side. From this position it's easy to do hand gestures, turn the upper body and face towards different parts of the room while at the same time remaining in the grounded position with a relaxed lower body.

The grounded posture is useful to adopt if you have a habit of swaying when speaking or moving weight restlessly from one foot to another. If you need to remain behind a lectern for an entire presentation it is possible to use the grounded posture to do this, moving your feet occasionally for comfort.

Grounded posture can also boost the voice, provided the upper body is held upright with open shoulders. An upright body has the spine, back and head aligned. One way to achieve this is to imagine a piece of string starting from the base of the spine (the lower back) and coming out of the top of your head. Keep your spine, back and head in line with the imaginary string. The breath moves in and out more efficiently with this alignment, which in turn improves the sound of the voice.

It is possible, and a good idea, to maintain a grounded posture when sitting down to speak. Keep your feet flat on the floor and sit upright. Do not rest your body against the back of a chair – make sure you are supporting your spine solely from your seated position. Keep your shoulders open and align your spine, neck and head.

Hands behind the back

I have never been a fan of presenting with hands held behind the back and I encourage speakers not to begin their speech with this posture. Maybe it's the military association that troubles me. It feels overbearing and often looks awkwardly stiff.

But there are other viewpoints on holding your hands behind the back. Allan and Barbara Pease say:

> The emotions attached to this gesture are superiority, confidence and power. The person exposes their vulnerable stomach, heart, crotch and throat in a subconscious act of fearlessness... if you take this position when you are in a high-stress situation... you'll begin to feel confident and even authoritative[29]

Move with purpose

Another way to come across as professional and credible is movement with purpose. If you choose to move around a stage, beware of nervous pacing. It's far better to be intentional when you move. This can be stepping forward from a central position and moving closer to the audience. Or it can be a walk from a central position to stage left or stage right or indeed walking across the entire stage.

Whatever the position, the idea is to make each movement tie into the structure of the presentation. For example, you might do the intro and first key point from centre stage; then the next key points at stage left and the subsequent key point stage right. You might choose to conclude by returning to centre stage position. This gives an evident point to movement.

Or you might want to keep movement minimal. In this case you could move from starting position into a second position to deliver a crucial bit of data or a story. Once you've communicated that content, you can return to the starting position for the rest of the presentation.

You can devise many different movement configurations to meet your requirements. With rehearsal it's straightforward to make the movements look poised, confident and professional.

Nerves

Nerves can overwhelm us and undermine credibility when speaking. At the same time, watching highly nervous speakers can be uncomfortable for an audience.

When nerves take over, a range of physical reactions are triggered. These include a faster heartbeat, rising blood pressure and perspiration. Tightness in the muscles in the neck and chest can make the voice wobble. Adrenaline rushes through the body.[30]

When in the grip of these reactions you do need rapid solutions to restore control. Slowing down the out breath and breathing deeply is a good place to start. (See page 75 for more on diaphragm breathing.)

Reducing nerves with Rag Doll

If nerves kick in well before you're on stage or in the board room, there is another useful technique called 'Rag Doll'.

Be aware that this activity looks a bit silly and so is best done in privacy. It's guaranteed to help release tension in the body and enable a speaker to control some of the physical symptoms of nerves.

Rag Doll

- Stand with your feet hip-width apart
- Keep your knees slightly bent and slowly bend over as if to touch your toes
- Keep your hands and arms loose and shake your shoulders from side to side 5–10 times (losing all stiffness in the body like a Rag Doll)
- Stand upright slowly to avoid feeling dizzy.

If you want more options on managing nerves, there's a whole chapter on the subject starting on page 179.

Body language to increase rapport with an audience

The best way to increase rapport is with eye contact. I have already discussed eye contact in the BRIBE model on page 36 so I won't repeat that information here.

I will discuss facial expression. The phrase 'fix your face' is something I heard when training as an executive coach. The person giving the advice was referring to the importance of being aware of facial expression when coaching a client. The point was how we look can impact the delicate nature of the client-coach relationship.

Audiences will look closely at the face of speakers. They are right to pay so much attention to facial expression. The face can communicate our deepest human emotions including fear, anger, sadness, happiness, disgust or surprise. These emotions are shown in movements of the mouth, eyes and eyebrows.

An expressive face can increase rapport when speaking but you need to be self-aware and not overdo it. A highly animated face can disconcert an audience and a facial expression that's too controlled may hamper rapport.

Smile

Some researchers say that smiling appears to start in the womb.[31] Others say that this universal human act starts in babies about five weeks old. In any case, babies work out that crying usually gets adult attention and smiling holds that attention.

Smiling continues to help with connection when we are adults making presentations. Furnham and Petrova note that:

> Smiling… is the outward manifestation of happiness, and serves to connect us to others… some researchers have shown that people who cannot smile, because of facial paralysis, say, have more difficulty in social relationships.[32]

When audiences see a speaker smile, they often respond by smiling themselves. They can't help it. Why? Well, you could say that smiling is contagious. The part of the brain responsible for smiling is an unconscious automatic response area called the cingulate cortex. A number of researchers have noted a mirroring effect where we automatically copy the facial expression of others we see.[33]

The act of smiling also makes speaker and audience feel better. It's to do with the way it stimulates the brain. There's the release of neuropeptides that reduce stress. The body relaxes and heart rate and blood pressure lower. The release of the neurotransmitters dopamine, endorphins and serotonin lift our mood. As you feel better you even want to smile more![34]

A smile directly affects how an audience relates to a speaker. 'People respond to those who smile, and evaluate them differently and more positively than those who do not.'[35]

Part of that positive speaker perception includes feeling a greater sense of trust and liking for the speaker and perceiving the speaker as more competent.[36]

For all these benefits, the smile can be problematic for women in business. It's likely the challenges start in childhood. From as early as two months old, baby girls smile more than baby boys. Then as adults women tend to smile more than men. Allan and Barbara Pease say that in social encounters, women smile 87% of the time versus 67% for men.

Researchers observe that powerful men smile less than powerful women. Researchers also found that pictures of unsmiling men were perceived as dominant while unsmiling women were perceived as unattractive.

BBC News anchor Martha Kearney says that earlier in her career a male boss told her she was too smiley for a top job in broadcasting. I am assuming that in the eyes of that BBC manager the female smile meant a less serious or less competent presenter. Fortunately, Martha Kearney disproved the stereotype by eventually landing the anchor role for the BBC's network radio breakfast show. It can be challenging for women whether they chose to smile or not.

Body language to increase the impact of a business message

In a presentation, gestures can help both audience and speaker. First the speaker. It's thought that gestures may be critical to a speaker. This is because gestures could be an essential component of speech rather than just something that adds emphasis to speech. The link is thought to be the fact that the part of the brain that controls speech and hand movements is located in the same place.[37]

This idea of gesture in spoken communication seems to be borne out when speakers try to restrict gestures. They find it's more challenging than expected and requires a lot of practice. They may even find gesture restriction interferes with the flow of speaking. This may also be due to the fact that we start to use hand gestures as infants. By adulthood, gestures have been integrated into our personality and communication style over many years.

Gestures that feel natural can help a speaker access memories and ideas while talking. A study that suggests this involved children and adults remembering information. Forty children and 36 adults were asked to remember a list of letters (adults) or words (children) while explaining how they solved a maths problem. Both groups remembered significantly more items when they gestured during their maths explanations than when they did not gesture.[38]

So why do gestures help us remember information when we're speaking? Memory expert Dr Fiona McPherson suggests this explanation:

> It's thought that gesturing helps memory and understanding by lightening the load on working memory while you're thinking of what to say. Gestures use up visuospatial working memory rather than verbal memory, so essentially what you're doing is moving part

of the information in one limited working memory space into another working memory space (and brain region).[39]

I don't like to prescribe gestures because if a speaker finds certain gestures uncomfortable or unfamiliar they won't work well anyway, at least not initially. I do like people to be aware of the gestures they use when speaking and assess the effect on audiences. Are the gestures helping to draw attention to words and ideas? Are they clarifying meaning? Recording and reviewing a rehearsal is a good way to assess this.

As you watch your movements, you might want to note the kind of gestures you are using and their impact. The three significant gestures presenters use are illustrators, regulators and adaptors.

- Illustrators – amplify what's being said. For example, hand gestures
- Regulators – control the audience in some way. For example, raising an arm to get an audience to be quiet
- Adaptors – these are anxiety displacements – these movements reveal the emotions of the speaker. For example, fiddling with a pen.[40]

Here are some common gestures used to increase impact in presentations.

- The Give – open two-handed gesture signalling and seeking trust
- The Show – hands wide apart in a big upward gesture. Useful in big conferences for creating energy and excitement
- The Chop – hand(s) moving quickly in a downward slicing action. Emphatic gesture
- Palm up – an open gesture commonly used when explaining ideas
- Palm down – conveys authority.

Beware of the closed palm and pointing finger. Audiences often find it irritating and even aggressive. Much better to use a pinched finger.[41]

I did say earlier that a speaker's gestures can help an audience. They help with audience recall, and research suggests they may increase recall by as much as a third.

A study exploring gesture and audience memory retention had participants watch cartoons with a person narrating alongside. Sometimes the narrator used hand gestures and at other times there were no gestures. The participants were then asked to recall the story. The study found that when the narrator used gestures and speech, the participants were more likely to accurately remember what actually happened in the story.[42]

Finally, audiences also send signals from their body language to a speaker. The body language of the audience can reveal what they think of the speaker and the presentation. Positive signals include sitting upright, a nod, smile or consistent eye contact. Slumped posture, avoiding eye contact, shuffling or folded hands can be negative signals that a speaker should observe and maybe respond to.

Summary

This chapter has discussed practical ways to use body language in presentations.

- To come across with more credibility
  - Pay attention to how you walk on
  - Use grounded posture
  - Move with purpose
  - Reduce nerves with Rag Doll.
- To achieve greater audience rapport
  - Give eye contact
  - Use facial expression

- ○ Smile.
- To get your message across with more impact
  - ○ Use gestures to help you remember ideas
  - ○ Use gestures to help your audience remember points
  - ○ Observe the body language of your audience and respond to it if necessary.

Reflective questions

- Does your walk-on excite an audience?
- Do you move around a stage with purpose?
- Do you need to smile more or less?
- What unconscious gestures do you use?
- What conscious gestures do you use?
- Are any of your gestures excessive?
- What new gestures do you want to try?
- How much eye contact do you give?
- How effective is your eye contact?
- How expressive is your face? How do you know?
- How are you using your hands when speaking?
- What is the audience body language telling you?

Chapter 9

SIGNATURE STYLE

Preview

THIS CHAPTER IS about increasing presence by developing a Signature Style. It covers:

- Reasons to develop a Signature Style
- The four elements of a Signature Style
  - The Presence Audit
  - Style principles
  - Colour confidence
  - Body shape
- The visual check

Reasons to develop a Signature Style

Clothes speak to an audience: in doing so they can make the presenter and they can undo the presenter. An attractively dressed speaker can generate positive impressions and perceptions of trust, likeability and competence in the critical early moments of a speech.

The appearance of a speaker also tends to reflect how she or he is feeling. I know if I am wearing accessories with tomato red or bright blue colours I am usually in a good place and excited about the presentation I am giving. I often choose darker or less intense colours if I am feeling more cautious.

The sorts of things that can diminish the presence of a speaker are:

- Clothes that are way too tight
- Baggy clothes that 'drown' the wearer
- Over-long jacket sleeves touching the finger tips
- Trouser lengths so long they crumple unattractively at the feet
- Colours (clothes, accessories) that overpower the speaker
- Colours (clothes, accessories) that are too pale and washed out for the speaker
- Too many competing colours (clothes)
- Make-up – overpowering
- Make-up – unflattering
- Clothes that seem too young for the speaker
- Clothes that seem to age the speaker
- Way too much jewellery.

The solution to many of these challenges is to develop a Signature Style. This means dressing to suit your personal colouring and body shape and at the same time communicating who you want to be. When you know your Signature Style, you have a benchmark for your appearance. You can turn the dial up for presentations if appropriate and move the dial down for less formal meetings or everyday workwear.

The Presence Audit

The starting point for creating a Signature Style is the Presence Audit – a three-word summary describing your ideal presence. Once you know your three words ask yourself how effectively is your appearance reflecting the Presence Audit. Use it to help you dress authentically and to manage your appearance. The way to create a Presence Audit is explained in full on page 70.

Defining Signature Style is an ongoing life-long process. Much like a handwritten signature, the fundamental style largely stays the same with changes resulting from age, circumstances and particular moods.

Defined style principles and qualities

Use style icons to identify the principles and qualities of your own Signature Style. Consider people whose style of dress you admire. They may be people you know, business executives or celebrities. There will be something about them that speaks to some aspect of your sense of self: your values, your style, your age, your work etc. My current icons are:

Michelle Obama

Her Signature Style evolved during her time as First Lady of the United States of America. Her wardrobe mixes fabulous designer clothes with high street outfits. Her clothes are often classic and elegant with a sense of fun, charisma, individualism and confidence.

Sheryl Sandberg – COO Facebook

Sheryl has a more minimalist style. Simple, elegant, clean lines. It's unfussy and uncluttered so there aren't many prints. The understated, high-quality look exudes confidence, professionalism and authority.

Audrey Hepburn

The Hollywood actress had a style partnership with French fashion designer, Givenchy, that gave the world so many examples of classically elegant and stylish clothes with exquisite simplicity.

Iris Apfel

She is the 90-something New York style queen who puts together the most wonderful outfits with eclectic designs and accessories. I find her individualism and originality liberating. She inspires me to have more stylistic fun.

Use style icons to clarify the principles, qualities and priorities of your Signature Style. Then use these principles to guide your appearance.

Colour confidence: Colour types

According to Coco Chanel, 'the best colour in the world is the one that looks good on you'. That sounds simple but it ain't easy. One method to work out your best colour is the concept of personal colouring using four colour types: light, deep, warm and cool.

While there's little hard evidence to confirm why one palette of colours is better suited to a particular skin colour, I know what I see with my own eyes. There's no doubt in my mind that some groups of colours look much better on people than others.

People often remark when a particular colour suits an individual. People may respond to the impact of a colour. For example, people might observe that an individual looks well and not necessarily be aware that they're noticing the effect of the colours worn by that individual.

The colours you wear *do* interact with your overall personal colouring and *do* get noticed by an audience so keep an open mind about adopting a colour palette based on personal colour types.

Knowing your personal colouring is the third step in developing a Signature Style. Determining your colour group may be something you can do yourself or something you can work out with help from a friend or colleague. However, it is not always straightforward and may even require the skilled eye of a professional image consultant or stylist.

I am about to give a highly generalised overview of colour types. The simplification is meant to get you started on the process of understanding and using colour palettes to manage your appearance. For the purposes of clarity and easy understanding we will work with four colour groups.

A colour expert works out personal colouring by looking at the overall colour impression that comes from the colour of a person's skin, eyes and hair. The four groups are:

- light cool (LC)
- light warm (LW)
- deep cool (DC)
- deep warm (DW).

Light or deep?

It's usually straightforward to know whether you have overall light or deep (darker) colouring. Look closely in the mirror in natural daylight to assess the combined colour effect of your hair, eyes and skin. Is it light or deep? If your hair is grey or greying, what colour was it when you were 21? As you assess hair colour do note that light-coloured hair can be anything from blonde, to mid-brown or even light red.

Warm or cool?

If you decide your personal colouring is *light* then the next thing to figure out is whether that lightness is more warm coloured or cool coloured. If you have warm colouring, ivory, peach and light camel colours suit your skin. Cool colouring goes better with dusty pink, raspberry or mid-greys.

Light colouring is either *light and cool* (LC) or *light and warm* (LW).

If you decide your personal colouring is *deep*, you also need to work out whether you fall into *deep and cool* (DC) or *deep and warm* (DW). When you look at your face and inside wrists do you see warm or cool undertones? Cool colouring suits magenta, dark navy, charcoal grey. Warm colouring suits teal, chocolate brown, peacock blue.

Ask people who know you to help if it's not immediately clear. It might also help to review the chart below of well-known people grouped into colour types.

Colour group	Examples of men	Examples of women	Colour
LC Light & cool	Tim Cook Daniel Craig Tom Hiddleston	Sienna Miller Helen Mirren Nicole Kidman	Bright navy, charcoal blue grey, soft white, clear taupe, medium grey, pastel pink
LW Light & warm	Prince Harry Damien Lewis Michael Fassbender	Kate Winslett Reese Witherspoon Cameron Diaz	Medium navy, peach, soft white, beige, ivory, cocoa, light warm grey
DC Deep & cool	George Clooney Idris Elba Aiden Turner	Meghan Markle Duchess of Cambridge Michelle Obama	Black, charcoal grey, dark navy, pure green, pure white, icy pink, icy blue

DW	Christian	Jennifer Lopez	Chocolate
Deep & warm	Ronaldo	Keira Knightley	brown, rust, camel, teal,
	Keanu Reeves	Jennifer	orange, olive
	Christian Bale	Aniston	green, beige, ivory, cream

Figure 10: Colour groups and palettes

In the fourth column of the table I've listed a few examples from the colour palettes that work with the four types. The colour groups are related to the palettes because they share the same properties. For example in the group *Deep Cool* (DC) the palette contains colours that are themselves deep and/or cool.

I do find colour groups and palettes helpful and most of the time I do stick to the deep and cool colours of my palette. However, I don't like to feel too harnessed to colours so I encourage you, sometimes, to wear colours you absolutely love. Yes, even if they are strictly speaking outside your colour palette. If you feel a colour is somehow integral to your personality you will feel great when you wear it so it may well have a place in your Signature Style. Consider getting a second opinion of the colour from a trusted friend. Also check how the colour looks against your face. Sometimes that helps to decide if it really suits you.

Colour confidence – colour combinations

Once you have a palette of colours that suit you, consider how to combine colours for different business situations. Colour combinations can make us seem more authoritative, attractive, modern, bold, creative, conservative or even boring!

A handy tool to discover new colours and new ways to combine colours is the colour wheel used by designers and advertising companies. It is literally a circular chart with 12 colours side by side: primary colours (red, yellow, blue), secondary colours (orange, green, violet) and tertiary colours (yellow-green, blue-green, blue-violet, red-violet, red-orange, and yellow-orange).

To see an example of a simple colour wheel visit: www.freepik.com/free-photo/basic-color-wheel_605995.htm

The colour wheel helps you work out new colours that mix well together. The mixes are created by the position of colours on the wheel. See some of the mixes below.

The monochromatic mix

This refers to colours in the same column in the wheel: they are different shades of exactly the same colour. An example of dressing this way is wearing a pale blue shirt and mid-blue trousers. The monochrome look is good for business casual. It smartens up the look and comes across as 'pulled together'.

The analogous mix

Analogous just means similar so these colours are next to each other on the wheel either as pairs or groups of three. Colours in this mix blend really well. The impact is harmonious and confident and stronger than the monochromatic mix.

The complementary mix

These colours are opposite each other on the wheel and create a vivid, contrasting effect. This mix is good for standing out from the crowd, for being bold. I remember being very excited when I used this mix by combining a fuschia jacket with a lime green camisole. It made a dramatic statement. I loved it.

The triadic mix

This is the combination of three colours that are evenly spaced around the colour wheel. For example, yellow, orange and pink (one space apart) or violet, orange and green (three spaces apart). There's no doubting the effect of these colours: they are vibrant even in soft shades. These colours might be combined in a print or pattern in accessories like a scarf or tie, or they could be elements or items of clothing. This mix is for high-impact dressing.

Neutrals

The neutrals are black, navy, grey, brown, cream, white. They mix well with any of the colours in the wheel. Neutrals also work well with each other. They are popular colour combinations for business as they look chic and professional. They are the sort of colours that say 'I am serious' although overuse of neutrals can look a little boring or anonymous.

Other points about colour

- Darker colours look more powerful and formal
- Bright colours, like tomato red, are high impact and grab attention
- Less intense hues have a softer impact and make you seem more approachable
- Pastels have a subtle, fresh effect
- Turquoise is universal. It's a mix of warm and cool colours so it suits everyone!

There is a brilliant interactive version of the colour wheel that's worth exploring. It lets you select a colour and automatically shows the different mixes described above. Go to: www.rapidtables.com/web/color/color-wheel.html

I must admit I also like using a physical colour wheel. If you want to buy a physical wheel there are different types available from retailers like Amazon. Ultimately, colour confidence is about wearing colours that suit you and make you feel good.

Body shape

The final component of a Signature Style is body shape. This means knowing your body shape and wearing styles to suit your shape. Be really honest with yourself about how you look *today*.

As previously, I am offering a highly simplified outline of body shapes to get you started: to give you some awareness of how this concept can enhance executive presence. We will work with four body shapes (regardless of gender):

- Upright triangle
- Inverted triangle
- Straight
- Large.

Use Figure 11 to work out your body shape. If you feel uncertain, go for the shape that applies to you more than any of the others.

Body shape	Characteristics in men	Characteristics in women
Upright triangle	Shoulders narrower than hips	Hips wider than shoulders
Inverted triangle	Shoulders wider than hips	Bigger shoulders than hips Large bust and narrower hips
Straight	Hips and shoulders are similar width	Hips and shoulders are similar width Body shape doesn't come in at the waist
Large	Typically more contoured shape than angular Waist can be the widest part of the body	Waist is the widest part of the body Hips and shoulders are similar width Can be curvy shape

Figure 11: Body shapes

Image professionals help clients look great by assessing body shape and using balancing techniques to highlight strong body features and diminish the impact of weaker features. Here are some balancing ideas for different body shapes.

Balancing techniques

Upright triangle

Men

✓ Give impression of wider shoulders by wearing double-breasted jacket

✓ Wear cutaway collars in shirts as they have a widening effect

✓ Wear lighter colours on top (e.g. light jacket, dark trousers).

Women

✓ Draw attention away from narrow shoulders with softly padded shoulders

✓ Wear longer line or loose jackets

✓ Layer tops and jacket

✓ Avoid skirts that are wide at the hips

✓ A-line skirts work well

✓ Go for softer, draping fabrics

✓ Tops with narrow horizontal lines make your shoulders look wider.

Inverted triangle

Men

- ✓ Wear jackets and shirts that emphasise the natural silhouette
- ✓ Draw attention from wider shoulders with single-breast jackets
- ✓ Wear wide-peaked lapels
- ✓ Avoid boxy-style jackets as they can give a bulky appearance
- ✓ Go for tightly woven fabrics.

Women

- ✓ Draw attention away from wider shoulders with V-neck tops
- ✓ Wear wide lapels on shirts
- ✓ Cigarette trousers, skinny jeans suit this shape
- ✓ Flared skirts balance narrow hips.

Straight body shapes

Men

- ✓ Choose stripes and checks to create width if required
- ✓ Can wear most trousers styles
- ✓ Can wear most suit styles
- ✓ Avoid baggy, shapeless clothes.

Women

- ✓ Choose stripes and checks to create width if required
- ✓ Can use draping fabrics to create appearance of curves
- ✓ A-line skirts give balance
- ✓ Round or Sweetheart necklines flatter this shape
- ✓ Avoid baggy, shapeless clothes.

Large body shapes

Men

- ✓ Single-breast jackets with vents have a slimming effect
- ✓ Wear well-cut jackets and suits
- ✓ Fewer colours have a slimming effect
- ✓ Lower-buttoning lapels have a slimming effect
- ✓ Pleated trousers are often more comfortable
- ✓ Draping fabrics suit the body shape
- ✓ Button-down shirts are flattering.

Women

- ✓ Single-breast jackets with single buttons have slimming effect
- ✓ Long-line lapels in jackets give impression of length

✓   Go for well-cut jackets and suits

✓   Fewer colours are slimming

✓   Dark colours for trousers and skirts have a slimming effect

✓   Wear brighter colours on top

✓   Wide V-line tops

✓   Long jewellery creates illusion of length

✓   Vertical patterns.

Of course there are lots more things you can do to flatter your body shape.[43]

The visual check

When you've decided on clothes for a presentation, consider doing a visual check. It's something theatrical actors always do, according to costume designer Tina Bicat.

> The actor will begin to work using the mirror... Actors have to be confident of the picture they present so that they can concentrate on the character they are playing.[44]

Similarly, for a business presenter the purpose of completing a visual check is to feel confident that their appearance is well-presented and consistent with their Signature Style.

A speaker's visual check should be done in the actual clothes they intend to wear for a presentation and in front of a full-length mirror. Once the visual check is done the presenter can focus on the audience and the message to be shared.

Use the visual check to scrutinise appearance and address any details that might detract from the presenter and the presentation. The sort of details that might need attention include:

- Untidy hair
- Dirty nails
- Chipped nail polish
- Unshaven face
- Bulky pockets full of coins or keys
- Stained clothes
- Creased clothes
- Loose threads
- Fallen hems
- White socks
- Dirty shoes.

My final point on Signature Style is the importance of posture. The phrase 'Wear it Well' comes to mind. Good posture includes holding an upright frame with shoulders open and down, and a straight spine – regardless of being in a standing or sitting position. A great appearance can improve presence while poor posture can undermine it.

Summary

So to recap, to create your Signature Style work on the following:

1. A Presence Audit – a three-word summary of who you want to be

2. Style principles derived from style icons

3. Knowing your colour type and its palette of colours

4. Awareness of body shape and the best ways to flatter it.

Reflective questions

- What three words are in your Presence Audit?
- How effectively does your appearance express your Presence Audit? What, if anything, needs to change?
- What colours embody your Presence Audit?
- Who are your style icons and why?
- What are your core style principles and qualities?
- When you're getting dressed, what colours do you love?
- What colours do you stay away from?
- Do you know what colours suit you?
- What are your triggers for wearing a new or different colour?
- Is there a connection between the colours you wear and your mood?
- When you look in the mirror is your personal colouring light or dark, warm or cool?
- Are the colours you're wearing good for online video meetings?
- What's your body shape?
- What balancing techniques flatter your body shape?
- How can you apply the relevant balancing techniques to business casual dressing?
- When is a power suit right for your meetings?
- When do you need a tie?
- What accessories create the impact you want?
- The visual check: when is the best time to do it?

Chapter 10

HEADSHOTS

Preview

THIS CHAPTER EXPLAINS how professional headshots can help executives form positive first impressions ahead of delivering a presentation or attending a meeting. It covers:

- How headshots help executive presentations
- Preparing for a photoshoot
- Four tips for great headshots from an award-winning photographer

How do headshots help executive presentations?

Many presentation situations actually require headshots.

If you are speaking at an external conference it's likely that information about the conference and speakers will be available on a website and may also be promoted through social media. More often than not, information about speakers includes headshots of them.

Ahead of investor presentations, board meetings, pitch presentations and so on, participants often go online to look up information about those attending. Many will go straight to LinkedIn profiles where they will also see headshots.

Internal meetings often have slide decks or handouts with headshots of speakers. A French global organisation I worked with always provided a participant list with headshots. The document was called a trombinoscope. Given that headshots are so widely used it makes sense to use pictures that are professional-looking, convey a positive impression of the person and exude executive presence.

Another reason for having good headshots is what research tells us. Studies show the strong influence derived from seeing photographs of an individual ahead of actually meeting them.

Furnham and Petrova[45] note that psychologists who focus on impression formation have a concept, mentioned earlier, called 'thin slices of behaviour'. This looks at the impressions formed by participants after seeing a still or moving image for less than five seconds: what I call the five-second window.

In one revealing piece of research, students were shown photographs of teachers before they started classes. The students were asked to evaluate the teachers based on viewing a photograph for less than five seconds. The evaluations prior to class 'correlated highly' with the ratings given to the same teacher at the end of the course. Furnham and Petrova describe this as 'an amazing ability to pinpoint other people accurately on a range of different personality and quality scales without any deliberate or conscious thought on our part'.[46]

It seems safe to assume that the same impression formation takes place all the time in business. Up-to-date headshots that come across well will help achieve a positive first impression to people who do not know you. That becomes even more important when we consider that the initial impression from photos can correspond closely with how you are perceived after an audience has actually met you.

This is why I recommend investing in professional headshots taken by an experienced photographer. Indeed, there are now a number of companies who specialise in professional headshots for LinkedIn profiles and other business needs.

With so many companies doing this work it can be challenging to know where to start. In my case I used a personal contact who I'd done a photoshoot with previously. If you don't have that, try recommendations from colleagues and friends. Failing that, it might be a case of visiting websites to see which photographers produce the kind of headshots you like.

Preparing for a photoshoot

Once you have the photographer sorted, it's useful to think about the brief to give them.

I recommend doing a Presence Audit to guide a photographer to take pictures that represent you positively, authentically and in a relevant way.

The Presence Audit is something I explain in full in the chapter on vocal presence on page 70. The Audit is a three-word summary describing your ideal presence: each word reflects a slightly different aspect of your presence. The three-word audit I am currently using is:

- Professional
- Confident
- Warm.

Work out the best words for your Presence Audit to help your photographer understand exactly how you want to come across. Use the Presence Audit on yourself to check that you are embodying the qualities in your facial expressions, your eyes and how you smile. I suggest scrutinising shots during the photoshoot to double-check that your images express the qualities of your Presence Audit.

In addition to the Audit it is worth reviewing your Signature Style before meeting a photographer. Knowing your Signature Style helps narrow decisions on clothes, accessories and personal grooming. Detailed guidance on how to determine your Signature Style is on page 99. In brief, the Signature Style consists of:

- Using style icons to identify your style principles and qualities
- Knowing your personal colour type and which colours make you look good
- Knowing your body shape and what styles flatter you.

It is true that 'we communicate our age, values, wealth and status by how we present ourselves to the world. We make a statement with our looks.'[47] Use the Presence Audit and Signature Style information to ensure that your headshots make a strong, intentional statement.

Once the brief is clear I suggest compiling a shot list if you want several different images. I wanted a number of images from my photoshoot for two reasons. I needed a variety of headshots to use across online platforms including blogs, website, LinkedIn and Twitter. It is also better value to get several images from one photo session.

I drew up a shot list so I was clear exactly how I wanted each headshot to look. My shot list read like this:

1. Smart: fresh and relaxed

2. Smart: corporate and interesting

3. Smart: vibrant

4. Relaxed: informal

In addition, I found it helpful to do a quick sketch of each look to organise packing clothes and accessories.

Each sketch contains a label summarising the impression I want to create and a description of clothes and jewellery required for the headshot. Below you can see how the sketches helped me achieve the look I wanted. I have placed the sketch beside the resulting headshot.

Smart: fresh and relaxed	Smart: fresh and relaxed
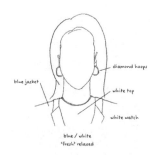	
Smart: corporate and interesting	Smart: corporate and interesting
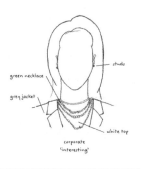	
Smart: vibrant	Smart: vibrant
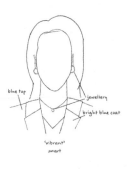	

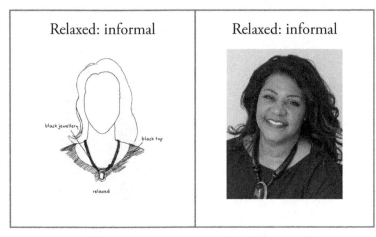

| Relaxed: informal | Relaxed: informal |

Figure 12: Headshots comparison

The shot list was only for my purposes and I did not show the photographer. I did, however, show the photographer a sample of five different headshots I had researched from the internet. They were pictures I thought worked well and would give the photographer a feel for what I wanted to achieve.

Award-winning photographer, Suzy Mitchell, took my headshots. Afterwards, I asked her advice on how to get great headshots.

Four tips for great headshots

It's about achieving a natural, engaging portrait: the best visual version of you, well photographed in beautiful light and which allows your personality to shine through. The most successful portraits are the ones where there is a connection between subject and photographer.

1) Leave plenty of time

Arrange the shoot for a time when you know you won't be under time pressure. Beforehand explain to your photographer what you will be using the images for and what you would like them to convey about you and your business.

2) Brand awareness

It's a good idea to see the shoot as an opportunity to enhance your personal branding. Give a little thought to the way in which you dress and where the photos will be taken if this is a location shoot. The environment in which you set your portrait can help tell the story of your business in a way that a simple shot against a white background will never be able to.

All the elements in the portrait should gel. For example, a lawyer will look right photographed in the library, in front of the court, with more sombre, muted colours in terms of clothing and buildings.

3) Hair!

This is a big one! Women, book a hair appointment! Don't do anything drastic as you need to look like you: a finished, polished look is what you are aiming for.

Wear some make-up too... this will help your photographs enormously. Remember your photographer can only do so much... they can put you in the right light, help with positioning of the body etc. but they can't overcome a badly fitting suit, poorly applied make up or a bad hair day.

Guys, think about your suit – is it clean and well cut? Shave (if you are normally clean shaven). Weigh up what you propose to wear: does it portray the real you and at the same time enhance your personal brand?

4) Find a photographer with whom you 'gel'.

Try to meet up beforehand or at the very least have a chat on the phone. Do they listen and are they receptive to your ideas? Are they willing to collaborate with you because at the end of the day you should see the process as just that, a collaboration.

Suzy Mitchell

Photographer

www.suzy-mitchell.com

Final tip

If you want to make sure you're using the best pictures of yourself, there's a free website called Photo Feeler where you can post your pictures and get feedback. The feedback can be quite illuminating. The website is: www.photofeeler.com

Summary

Headshots help executive presentations by providing a positive first impression well before you start speaking. Headshots will be seen by people who receive speaker profiles or who research speakers before a presentation. Studies suggest that the impressions formed in the first few seconds of seeing an unknown headshot correlate closely with the judgements formed after actually meeting the speaker. Of course, this is not true of speakers already known to audiences. In this case, the headshots will reinforce or undermine existing impressions of a speaker.

You can prepare a brief for a professional shoot by completing a Presence Audit and clarifying your Signature

Style. Use the information to tell a photographer exactly how you want to come across.

Putting together a shot list with a sketch and labels can help with organising clothes and accessories.

Remember, a good headshot is about creating the best visual version of you.

Reflective questions

- What overall statement do you want your headshots to make?
- What values do you want your headshot to communicate?
- What message about your work do you want the headshots to articulate?
- How will your Presence Audit inform the headshots?
- How will your Signature Style inform the headshots?
- How will you choose a photographer?
- What will you use the headshots for?
- How many different headshots do you need?
- Do you need a shot list to organise clothes and accessories?
- Do you need to visit a hairdresser/barber beforehand?
- Make-up: do you need to practise applying make-up or book a make-up artist?

Chapter 11

THE ATTITUDE OF GRATITUDE

P RACTISING GRATITUDE HAS been described as the 'the ultimate performance-enhancing substance!'[48] See what you think when you get to the end of this chapter.

Preview

This chapter covers:
- How gratitude helps nerves
- How gratitude improves personal presence
- How gratitude helps connection
- Ways to practise gratitude

A few questions for you to consider as a speaker:

Do you have a positive presence?

Do you feel calm when addressing an audience?

Do you feel happy?

Do you manage your nerves well?

Do you feel resilient to cope with the unexpected?

Do you connect well with your audience?

I hope the answer is yes to all the above but if not the attitude of gratitude might be a solution.

The daily practice of gratitude can help a speaker to conquer nerves, develop a positive presence and connect well with an audience. These messages are coming from university researchers and neuroscientists. They are telling us that practising gratitude is something business leaders really should pay attention to. In this book my focus is on how gratitude helps leadership communication but there are businesses around the world using gratitude to strengthen corporate culture and improve performance. They consider gratitude a critical element to achieving a high-functioning organisation.[49]

As a Yorkshire lass, I love effective tools that are free so that's another reason for my enthusiasm for the practice of gratitude.

I should say that my interest in gratitude is relatively new and was inspired by my INSEAD colleague, Steve Knight, who uses it to develop vocal power. I was initially bemused at the prospect of teaching executives how to use gratitude in spoken communication. I always thought of gratitude as some sort of religious practice or philosophical pursuit – and of course it is! It wasn't immediately clear to me what specific activities expressing gratitude involved and how it would ever help anyone giving executive presentations. In my attempt to find out I discovered there are plenty of resources.

One excellent source of information on gratitude comes from the world of positive psychology which studies the science of human flourishing.[50] Positive psychology is interested in getting evidence to measure the effectiveness of expressing gratitude. If you are curious about this you might want to read research by Robert Emmons at the University of California at Davis (totally irrelevant but I was a student there!) or visit the Greater Good Science Center website – part of UC Berkeley.[51]

These sources give science-based information about the wide-ranging benefits of being grateful. They are remarkable and include increased well-being, feeling happier, being calm, feeling resilient and better social interaction. Indeed, it seems that these benefits can also be long-lasting.

Technological developments in neuroscience (particularly the use of the fMRI scanner) are also giving new insights into gratitude. Researchers can now see what the brain is doing when we express gratitude and it seems the brain has a distinctive area of its own that functions when we express gratitude. Scientists have observed that the effects of expressing gratitude can last weeks or months.[52]

All in all I found compelling information about the value of practising gratitude for business leaders.

Gratitude helps nerves

Help me get rid of nerves! This crops up frequently on the wish list of my workshop participants. When answering I often refer executives to physical techniques discussed in the middle section of this book – for example, diaphragm breathing. Participants sometimes raise eyebrows when I also suggest that expressing gratitude can help control nerves.

I jokingly illustrate the link between thought and deed by saying that when I express gratitude for my husband I am a lot nicer to him throughout the day!

And when it comes to high-stakes presentations I get nervous like everybody else. I know I have a tendency to be hypervigilant so even when I am well prepared for a presentation I can still feel quite anxious. I have noticed that if I express gratitude it does cut down those nerves. In practice this means I tell myself *why* I am grateful to be doing a particular presentation.

It could be any of the following:
- I am grateful for the opportunity to share ideas with my audience

- I am grateful to help others find their voice
- I am grateful for the opportunity to learn from my talented audience
- I am grateful to keep developing my presentation skills.

Before a presentation I usually think these things in my head and that's often enough to calm me down. If I am particularly anxious, I might state out loud my gratitude. If I am feeling extremely challenged, I write down what I am grateful for. There seems to be something significant about writing down feelings of gratitude. Later in this chapter I return to the importance of expressing gratitude in written form. See page 134.

So what's causing the breakthrough in my nerves? A technique called reframing is certainly one explanation. Reframing is a well-known and well-used coaching technique. I use it in my own work as a communication coach. My colleagues at the Hudson Institute of Coaching describe it rather well when they say that reframing:

> Changes the meaning of a belief or experience to shift attention to consider a new perspective or possibility.[53]

So the simple act of expressing gratitude ahead of a challenging presentation helps me shift my focus from my internal anxiety. My mind instead turns to the potential positive outcomes of my presentation. If this sounds a bit unlikely, all I can say is that it works for me.

American social psychologist Amy Cuddy similarly describes reframing nerves in her book on *Presence*. She says that in a challenging situation, instead of telling yourself to calm down beforehand it's better to harness the nervous energy and reframe it as excitement. She says:

By nudging ourselves from anxiety to excitement – we shift our psychological orientation, harnessing the cognitive and physiological resources we need to succeed under pressure. We effectively transform our stage fright into stage presence.[54]

Gratitude helps presence

Our presence is obviously affected by our mental and physical health and practising gratitude can contribute to both. Let's start with the benefits to mental health described in one study.

Participants who took part in gratitude research were asked to write letters of gratitude. They reported developing a significantly more grateful disposition two weeks after the task. They also reported feeling better mental health 4–12 weeks after they finished the task of writing a daily gratitude journal for 21 days.[55]

Robert Emmons, the noted researcher in gratitude, points to the positive outlook that gratitude generates when he says: 'Gratitude produces higher levels of positive emotions that are beneficial in the workplace, such as joy, enthusiasm and optimism.'[56]

He refers to social psychological research that indicates 'when people are experiencing gratitude they are approximately 20-30% less likely to be annoyed, irritated and aggressive'.

Perhaps the data I find most interesting is to do with character strengths. Robert Emmons reveals that out of 24 character strengths, love of learning and gratitude were the strongest predictors of overall well-being.[57]

In addition to how we think and feel, there's also research pointing to the physical effects of gratitude. Jeff Huffman compared the health of patients who survived a heart attack. They were divided into groups of those who practised gratitude and those who did not. He concluded from the comparison that:

> Gratitude might also have beneficial biological effects that help the cardiovascular system and overall health. Studies of various measures of positive psychological well-being, from happiness to optimism to gratitude, have found that experiencing well-being more frequently and more strongly is associated with lower levels of inflammation throughout the bloodstream and the body, a calmer fight-or-flight autonomic nervous system, and other effects that are clearly linked with better prognosis and longer survival. Beyond momentary happiness or pleasure, there is some suggestion that deeper well-being — like having life satisfaction, gratitude, and a sense of life purpose — might have much stronger effects on long-term health.[58]

Gratitude can help with connection

Connecting to an audience is one hallmark of effective executive presentations and that connection can be enhanced with the practice of gratitude.

Neuroscientists have told us that expressing gratitude generates activity in a specific area of the brain which has a small overlap with empathy and altruism.[59] That physical closeness perhaps explains why the act of gratitude increases our empathic behaviour. The Kini et al. research concludes that gratitude enhances empathy and affects our interactions with other people in that we are 'more willing to act in a way that has a positive impact on others'.[60]

Researchers call the increased connection with colleagues that comes with gratitude 'prosociality'. It means that people with a strong practice of gratitude have the capacity to be more empathic and to understand the perspective of others.

They are also described as more generous and more helpful by people in their social networks.[61]

Ways to *practise* gratitude

So what does practising gratitude involve? Saying a prayer is one form, as people of faith have done for hundreds of years. Below is a prayer of thanksgiving from the Church of England, originally from the 1662 prayer book.

> Almighty God, Father of all mercies, we your unworthy servants give you humble thanks for all your goodness and loving-kindness to us and to all whom you have made.
>
> We bless you for our creation, preservation, and all the blessings of this life; but above all for your immeasurable love in the redemption of the world by our Lord Jesus Christ; for the means of grace, and for the hope of glory.
>
> And, we pray, give us such an awareness of your mercies, that with truly thankful hearts we may show forth your praise, not only with our lips, but in our lives, by giving up ourselves to your service, and by walking before you in holiness and righteousness all our days; through Jesus Christ our Lord, to whom, with you and the Holy Spirit, be honor and glory throughout all ages.

Other ways to practise include:

Self-talk

As mentioned earlier, I often say to myself the specific things I am grateful for before a challenging presentation. Sometimes this is in the preparation phase and sometimes it is just before I speak at an event.

Gratitude journal or letter

Lots of research has been conducted using written journals or gratitude letters so we know they are particularly effective. One study mentioned earlier gets participants to write a journal for a period of 21 days and found it produced benefits lasting up to three months.

So, how about a 21-Day Gratitude Challenge to complete a daily writing journal? Take the opportunity each day to reflect on the things you are grateful for.

I appreciate that writing by hand is a little old school for some so you could use word-processing software on your phone or tablet.

Gratitude app

There are so many gratitude apps. Enjoy browsing to find one that works for you.

Gratitude meditation

Again, there are a variety of apps and sites that can assist with this. I liked the 10-minute guided mediation I downloaded by Dr Kathi Kemper at Ohio State University's Center for Integrative Health and Wellness. It's designed to promote resilience through heart-centred gratitude. To listen go to: https://wexnermedical.osu.edu/~/media/Files/WexnerMedical/Patient-Care/Healthcare-Services/Integrative-Medicine/MP3-Files/Heart-Centered-Practices/Gratitude-2.mp3?la=en

If would like to follow the script or use it with colleagues go to this link: https://ggia.berkeley.edu/practice/gratitude_meditation

So, as we end the chapter I return to the opening comment. Do you think the practice of gratitude might become your performance-enhancing substance of choice?

Summary

Practising gratitude is a relatively simple technique that can help speakers in big ways.

- Use it to handle nerves
- Use it to improve presence both physically and mentally
- Use it to connect more empathically to colleagues and audiences.

Reflective questions

- What are you grateful for in your life?
- What are you grateful for today?
- What are you grateful for right now?
- What form of expressing gratitude appeals to you?
- Is gratitude a new habit you want to commit to?
- Will you start a 21-day challenge to write a gratitude journal?
- How do you want gratitude to help your executive presentations?

Chapter 12

SELF-COACHING

Preview

This chapter is about developing presence with self-coaching techniques. You will learn:

- How to increase chances of successful change
- How to leverage the superpower of attention
- Self-awareness techniques
- How to do a mental rehearsal

I once worked with a client who my American friends might describe as 'the real deal'. She was a smart, attractive, experienced and effective leader. Yet when it came to her presentations she was always disappointed. There were no disastrous presentations – they just didn't reflect her talent and personality.

We started an executive coaching engagement and it eventually emerged that as a young child an incident at school remained with her even as she became a successful leader. The event left her feeling that she wasn't good enough and never would be, and this belief was particularly overwhelming when she was presenting. Powerful stuff. She worked really hard to challenge the negative belief she was holding on to and eventually made great progress with her presentations.

Here's my question to you. Is there something holding you back from excelling in your presentations? Is it something you can't quite identify? Or is it something you know only too well?

You may have the opportunity to work with a communication coach, like my client, or there is another option: self-coaching. It involves learning tools so you can coach yourself. You're probably your best coach anyway. As this is another free technique, like gratitude, you know I'm all smiles.

This self-coaching chapter is inspired by the work of my coaching colleague and fellow author, Mike Normant, who is based in San Francisco. He has developed an impressive self-coaching programme called *Coach Yourself Up*. It is thoughtful, effective and relatively straightforward to do. If you want to follow the full programme take a look at his website: http://coachyourselfup.com

How self-coaching helps

Executives can benefit in several ways from the coaching techniques in this chapter.

- You can learn to be more present when speaking in public
- You will focus attention more effectively on yourself and your audience
- You will work on beliefs that hold you back
- Increased attention will help you be more productive when preparing presentations.

The self-coaching work in this chapter involves developing attention, increasing self-awareness and mental preparation. There are nine exercises to do and I recommend starting a journal to record answers to the questions in the exercises. The journal is also a good place to notice patterns of behaviour and track progress.

Increase success

We can increase the success of long-term change by framing goals in the context of aspiring to be our best self.[62] The Presence Audit discussed earlier uses this idea. The Audit is a three-word summary describing our ideal presence. The process for conducting a Presence Audit is described in full on page 70.

If you have already done a Presence Audit, review it to make sure it still reflects exactly who you want to be as a leader. If you haven't done one yet, do any of the words below belong in your Presence Audit?

creative	confident	dynamic	inspiring
engaging	authentic	visionary	clear
decisive	approachable	articulate	warm

Use your Presence Audit to guide your development as you go through the self-coaching exercises. It is the outcome for the changes you want to make.

Another point to bear in mind on the self-coaching journey is time. For years I have worked in newsrooms where everything needed to be done yesterday! It has taken me years to adjust my internal clock. My training as an executive coach changed my time frame. The development work with clients can take anything from a couple of months to 18 months. This is because long-lasting change requires practice and persistence and yet more practice.

As you get going on coaching yourself hold on to the fact that coaching is not a quick fix. It may take several months to get close to your goal.

Managing attention

Managing attention is an idea that's new to me so I have been testing it out. It's given me useful insights into triggers that cause me to be irritated, angry or frustrated. It also strikes me as highly valuable for becoming more present when speaking.

In fact, Mike Normant confidently declares that 'attention is a superpower for life'. This is partly because when you have more awareness of your attention it increases your presence. It deepens the connection to self, to colleagues and makes for highly effective executive presentations.

Cultivating this superpower is quite a challenge in our modern age of emails, texts and messaging. There are constant distractions and interruptions occurring throughout the working day. Despite our best efforts, how often does our attention wander in long conference calls, over-running board meetings and tiring team meetings?

I love the headline that 'Humans have shorter attention span than goldfish'.[63] The subsequent article discusses a Canadian study by Microsoft revealing that between the years 2000 and 2016 the average human attention span has fallen from 12 seconds to eight seconds. (Oh, and in case you're wondering, goldfish are supposed to have an attention span of nine seconds!)

The article suggests one solution is reducing activity on smartphones. That would certainly help. However, learning how to hold our attention requires more than switching off a phone. We need to be more aware of our attention and what it's doing in order to have any control over it. That's exactly the work of the following exercises on attention.

Exercise 1: Notice attention

Our attention moves in and through our mind, our body and our world. A good exercise to show this is to sit still for

30 seconds. Keeping your eyes open just notice where your attention goes. Don't try to manage your attention, just let it go wherever.

- Where did your attention go in that time?
- What kind of experience was this for you?

When I did this exercise sitting in my office in the countryside, my attention roamed all over the place. It moved so often without me. It is no wonder that it's so hard to pay attention. During the exercise I noticed:

- The image on my computer screen
- Birds chirping outside
- The sound of a car engine
- An aeroplane engine
- My hands on my lap
- Tightness in my jaw
- Thoughts about my book deadline
- Thoughts about groceries for dinner
- Thoughts about my son
- A pen on my desk
- A book on my shelf.

Exercise 2: Direct attention

Now you're noticing what's constantly happening to your attention, it's time to move on to the superpower stuff of *directing* attention.

A good way of learning this is to listen to a recording by Gary Sherman,[64] an expert on the concept of expanding human potential by developing attention. Sherman neatly guides you through an eight-minute activity that gets you to focus attention on different locations. The download is free so do try it: www.mechanicsofawakening.com/free-downloads. html

In the activity you focus attention for about ten seconds. As previously noted, the average person's attention span is eight seconds (page 140) so this might be challenging at first. I certainly found it so.

- How did you find this activity?

Exercise 3: Direct your own attention

Ready to try self-directing your attention?

Sit still for one minute. In that time focus your attention on your mind for about ten seconds and then shift attention to your body and then to the world around you. Then go back to your mind, body and world – each time for approximately ten seconds.

Try it a few times.

- What was this experience like for you?

Developing attention develops self-awareness. You become more aware of when your attention moves away and when you need to guide it back. You might also start to become more aware of your thoughts and behaviours and how your body responds in different situations.

Exercise 4: Meditation

Meditation is regarded by many as a practice for increasing the management of attention. I've been meditating since 2015. I start my working day with a short meditation: sometimes silent, sometimes guided, sometimes with music. I started the practice to relax and 'tune in' to myself.

Meditation could aid your progress in managing attention. I encourage you to try it for two weeks to see what it does for you.

- What happens to you when you meditate?

- What emotions do you feel?

If you want to continue the practice of meditating, there are many meditation apps available so do explore. My favourite websites for listening to meditation podcasts are:

www.headspace.com

www.meditationoasis.com/podcast/

Exercise 5: Single tasking

The task is to watch a short video called 'Single Tasking is the new Multitasking' (less than five minutes' long). It's about focusing attention on one task at a time rather than multitasking. This is relevant to preparing presentations. In my experience, many people don't prepare effectively. Work is done at the last minute, and not given enough time or attention. When doing presentation preparation, single tasking could help get more done more efficiently.

The link to the video is: https://vimeo.com/98743711

- What do you think of the video message?
- Will you start single task practice?
- Will you prepare your next presentation in single task mode?

Self-awareness

So far we have looked at strengthening our ability to focus attention to form deeper connections when speaking to people.

We now turn to personal stories and beliefs. These are quite different from the storytelling devices we have discussed in earlier parts of the book. These stories define how we see ourselves and how we behave. Some generate negative beliefs. All of us carry them around and they serve an important purpose in helping us understand the world around us. As Pamela McLean of the Hudson Institute says, 'we are meaning making machines – we can't help it'. However, some stories stop us being fully present and effective speakers.

It's these stories I want to work on next in our self-coaching journey. These stories can be difficult to tackle because we might not be aware of them if they are in a blindspot. Often it's easier to start identifying behaviours before stories and beliefs.

Seek the opinions of colleagues, friends and loved ones. Ask them about things you do habitually when presenting that don't serve you well. You might want to show them the following list to see if they have noticed any of the behaviours in you.

I have listed some typical self-limiting behaviours connected to presentations.

- Not listening to feedback
- Not implementing feedback
- Not doing enough preparation
- Always preparing at the last minute
- Over-preparing (rare!)
- Not speaking clearly
- Not speaking loudly enough
- Speaking with a monotone voice
- Speaking too quickly
- Not looking at the audience
- Not working on building rapport with an audience
- Not smiling when presenting
- Not pausing enough when speaking
- Always dreading presentations
- Not rehearsing important presentations
- Never feeling confident doing presentations
- Blaming others when presentations go wrong
- Not communicating with your body
- Gripping tightly onto a podium.

It's not an exhaustive list but hopefully it will get you started on seeing your own self-limiting behaviours. The key thing to note is that we are addressing behaviours – what you do in meetings and conference rooms.

Exercise 6: Self-limiting behaviours

- Write down all the self-limiting behaviours that you do
- Review input from friends and colleagues
- Identify the most significant behaviour for you.

As you choose the most significant behaviour, focus on one you'd love to change; focus on a behaviour that happens often (maybe several times a week); focus on a behaviour that would make a big impact on your presentations.

Once you've written down your self-limiting behaviour it's time to rewrite it in the powerful language of aspiration. See the following example:

1. Self-limiting behaviour: *I speak too quickly*

2. First draft of goal: *I want to speak more slowly*

3. Rewritten aspirationally: *I speak engagingly to colleagues/audiences.*

Over the next few weeks start noticing your self-limiting behaviour.

- How often does it occur in the course of a day or week?
- How much time is there between its occurrence and when you notice it? (*The belief is that the more you notice your SLB (self-limiting behaviour) the shorter the time between occurrence and awareness.*)

Remember, the purpose of this activity is purely to get you to *notice* your behaviour/patterns and bring them more clearly into your awareness and conscious mind. The more time spent 'noticing' often increases the chance of actually succeeding in changing the behaviour.

Getting to know our beliefs

The self-limiting things we do are generated from emotions, which themselves are generated from beliefs. Executive coaches often use the Ladder of Inference[65] to help clients understand their behaviour.

Using the image of a ladder, at the bottom of the ladder is observable data (things we see) and at the top of the ladder is the action we take to respond to that data (our behaviour). Without realising it, quite a lot happens between seeing something happen and responding to it. We filter or process the observed data and then we add meaning to that filtered data. We then make assumptions based on the meaning we created, and draw conclusions and check our adopted beliefs about the world before taking action based on those beliefs.

Let me share a short story of my own to illustrate a belief.

I vividly recall giving a speech in a large college auditorium when a woman from near the front suddenly stood up and left the hall. She walked down the central aisle while I was speaking – her heels clacking loudly on the wooden floor. At the time I was a little startled that she got up in the middle of my speech. I worried I wasn't doing a good job and felt anxious. This led to me momentarily losing my stride and then recover.

I now see that episode in a new light using the Ladder of Inference. Use Figure 13 and remember to start at the bottom of the table in the box titled 'Observable data'.

LADDER OF INFERENCE

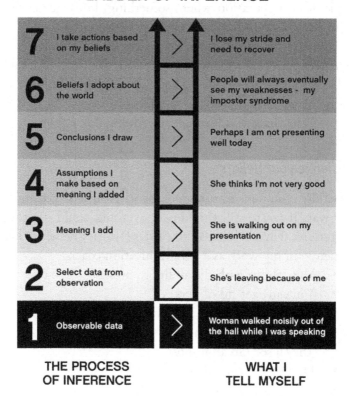

Figure 13: The Ladder of Inference

After the speech I learned the woman's departure had nothing to do with me: she was leaving early for childcare reasons. My worry was completely unnecessary! The insight that emerged from the Ladder of Inference was the story/belief controlling my behaviour. The story limiting me was that I was an imposter and not good enough.

Exercise 7: Challenge beliefs

Think of a presentation where something didn't go so well. Write down an outline of the event in your journal.

Now try to break down the event using the stages of inference. You might like to capture it in the form of a table as above – peeling away all the layers of thinking until you see clearly the belief that's getting in your way.

- What have you learned from doing this activity?

Challenge your beliefs

Hopefully you are starting to identify beliefs getting in your way. If you're still thinking it over and could use some suggestions, have a look at the list of stories/beliefs I hear frequently in my work as a communication coach.

- You're born with the ability to present
- You can't get rid of nerves
- I've tried everything – nothing works
- I'll never be good enough
- They'll see I'm an imposter
- I'm not smart enough
- I'm not successful enough
- They want me to fail
- I will always hate presenting
- I'm too shy
- I'm not charismatic
- I'm not an extrovert
- I'm not a performer
- Presenting is not really my thing
- I'm never happy with my presentations
- I have to be perfect
- I need to be seen as a successful speaker
- I have to prove myself all the time
- It's too late to improve my speaking skills

- I always beat myself up after a presentation
- People don't listen to me
- I can't speak in front of an audience
- I need to be liked by everybody
- People won't like the real me
- Being vulnerable is weak
- Something will always go wrong.

If you're starting to pinpoint your story or belief, the next step is to challenge it. The Ladder of Inference can certainly help. Alternatively, try asking yourself the following series of useful questions to interrogate a self-limiting belief. I used them to challenge my belief that 'people will always see my weakness – my imposter syndrome'.

Crucial conversation questions

- What specific feelings connect to this story? (Be as precise as you can)
- What evidence is there to support this story?
- Am I stepping into the role of victim/helpless person?
- What's my contribution to this story?
- What do I really want?
- What would I do if I really wanted these results?[66]

Say your name!

And here's another set of questions to try. Mike Normant has some great challenging-story questions. He also suggests using your *name* in the question so you address yourself in the third person. It's based on research[67] that indicates we can be more successful when dealing with our emotions when we use language that makes us a more detached observer.

As always, I test these ideas and I *really* like this one. See the following challenging questions and how I might say them if I were doing them.

- How do you know that to (always) be true, Jacqui?
- What other valid stories could one create based upon the same observable data, Jacqui?
- How might you act differently, Jacqui, if you didn't believe this story to be true?
- Do you think it would serve you to act that way, Jacqui?
  (should always be a resounding 'yes')
- How will you experiment with acting differently,[68] Jacqui?

Exercise 8: Challenge stories

Practise interrogating your stories with any of the techniques above (Ladder of Inference, Crucial Conversation questions or Say Your Name questions). Write down your answers.

- What did you notice as a result of the exercise?

Mental rehearsal: What is it?

The final concept in this self-coaching chapter is a tool much-used by elite athletes to achieve best performance in highly competitive situations: mental rehearsal. Some call it mental imagery or mental management. Away from the track or field, athletes literally think through the actions of their sport, moment by moment, experiencing it in their minds as vividly as possible. It's this that helps them achieve personal bests and win championships.

A good way of understanding how mental rehearsal affects performance is a computer analogy where software is the mind and hardware is the body. The software controls how well the hardware operates. Elite athletes have high-performing software that helps them use their hardware to the best of its ability.[69]

Mental imagery has been used in top-level sport for some 50 years and is now widespread. At the 2014 Winter Olympics the American team had 93 athletes and nine sports psychologists.[70] There are amusing images of athletes zoning out while doing mental rehearsals, often moving their hands. The American team were not alone in doing this. Many competing countries also brought along sports psychologists for their athletes.

It's thought that mental rehearsal fires the same brain cells that are actually involved in doing an activity, whether it's sport or communication. There are many compelling studies showing the beneficial effects. A recent one is described in *Military Medicine*. It describes how the American Military trialled a sports psychology programme for six weeks as part of preparation for fitness assessments for soldiers. It included mental imagery or mental rehearsal. The company of soldiers scored up to 14 points higher after sports psychology training than previously. The American Army is now looking at implementing sports psychology in its fitness preparation for soldiers throughout the army, and especially those in the early stages in their career.[71]

Can this process help with preparing executive presentations? It is certainly worth exploring. It could be said that executives delivering high-stakes presentations face some of the challenges of elite performers. When delivering important messages, executives need to be confident, focused, highly motivated and highly engaged while under pressure – much like professional athletes.[72]

Three ways to do a mental rehearsal

The mental rehearsal can be done a couple of days before a big presentation, on the day of a major presentation or even just a few minutes before. Experiment to find what works best for you after looking at the three methods below.

Mental rehearsal – Method 1

1. Choose a space where you will not be disturbed and where you can lie down or rest comfortably.

2. Close your eyes and relax your body. Start to focus your mind inwards.

3. Breathe in deeply and breathe out slowly. On the out breath start to release stress from your body. Focus on your feet first, then legs, then chest, then the top of your head. It's time to remove all distractions and let your mind relax.

4. Once relaxed, gently turn your attention to the presentation.

5. Speak to your mind. Mentally tell yourself that you are confident and that you can do a successful presentation. With self-confidence repeat to yourself several times that you will succeed.

6. Imagine, in as much detail as you can, what you will see just before you begin presenting. Visualise yourself actively engaged in speaking to an audience. Imagine that you are actually standing at the podium rather than watching yourself from the gallery.

7. Remaining relaxed and focused, mentally rehearse a successful presentation. Imagine going through the whole process and seeing highly successful results.

8. Repeat the previous step several times.

9. Finally, open your eyes and smile brightly. You have successfully performed a presentation in your mind, which is great preparation for an actual speech. You should now be confident that you will perform successfully in the real presentation. Remember to praise yourself for being successful as self-reinforcement is an important key to self-motivation.[73]

Mental rehearsal – Method 2

1. Focus on the aspects of your presentation that you really want to do well

2. Emphasise the *feeling* of presenting by referencing all of the senses that you can (see, hear, touch, taste, smell)

3. Create that image several times

4. Imagine everything around you including the conference hall, stage, podium etc.

5. Include strategies for highly successful presentations in the image

6. Finish with positive self-talk.[74]

Mental rehearsal – Method 3

One interesting additional element in the following American Military example is the inclusion of a script to say out loud. It gives a highly detailed account of the event you are preparing for. Some athletes record the script and play it back while relaxing.

Here is a copy of an imagery script from the American fitness assessment programme for push-ups. After completing the mental rehearsal, soldiers do their actual fitness assessment.

You are standing in line for the push up event. The air is crisp and smells of freshly cut grass. The temperature is cool.

Your arms are strong and you are ready. You take in a slow deep breath, in to the count of five and out to the count of five.

You are called up to begin the push up event. You get down into the front leaning rest position. The grass is moist and soft.

You position your hands comfortably and wait for the start.

You hear ready on the right, the right is ready; ready on the left, the left is ready. Ready – begin. Down and up, your arms feel strong and you are confident. Your form is good. You hear 1 minute has elapsed. Your arms are strong and steady and you are near your goal. You hear 30 seconds remaining. You continue up and down, breathing in on the way down and out on the way up. The final 10 seconds count down begins and you push out a few more. The event is over; you have done your best.[75]

Exercise 9: Mental imagery script

- Now write your own imagery script for a presentation incorporating the kind of ideas and detail in the military example above.

Summary

This self-coaching chapter included a collection of techniques to support your journey to mastery as a presenter. The ideas encourage you to:

- Increase your chances of success by creating a Presence Audit to lean into an ideal self
- Strengthen mental focus and attention – it is the stuff of champions and elite performers

- Challenge negative personal stories or beliefs
- Explore mental rehearsals to make your presentations even more successful.

Reflective questions

- How are you feeling about coaching yourself?
- Are you ready to commit to self-coaching?
- What strong beliefs do you have about yourself as a presenter? Which ones limit you? Which ones do you want to challenge? What feedback do you repeatedly get about your presentations?
- What do you fear most when speaking?
- What do you most want to change about your presentations?
- Which presentation have you been most proud of? Why?
- Which presentation did you find most difficult? Why?
- Where can you get inspiration from?

Chapter 13

PITFALLS AND SOLUTIONS

Preview

This chapter looks at the following common presentation pitfalls and how to avoid them:

- The speaker doesn't connect enough to the audience
- The message needs more impact
- The speaker lacks stage presence
- Online presence is underwhelming
- The slides are uninspiring

A note to readers starting the book here: throughout the chapter I have inserted page references to other parts of the book indicating specific topics I have discussed earlier and usually in more detail.

Not enough connection to the audience

Connecting to an audience is not an important aspect of a presentation – it is the most important aspect. Without strong connection there is no opportunity to gain trust, inform, enlighten or influence and precious time is wasted. It's not easy to achieve but it can be done using our body, words and emotions.

Emotions to help connection

Emotions will always be the place to start: the emotions of the speaker and the emotions of the audience. I encourage my executives to be passionate speakers because where the speaker leads, emotionally, the audience will follow. In my mind a passionate speaker is someone who cares deeply about their message and their audience. Experiencing a passionate speaker typically helps the audience to connect more quickly to the presenter.

I'm not talking about a highly impassioned speaking style as that can be problematic for an audience in a business environment.

When I hear executives say of their presentations 'I know this is boring' I warn them that if they feel their content is boring, so will the audience. It is our responsibility as effective communicators to unlock the passion in even the most unpromising topics.

I have seen highly absorbing presentations on unlikely technical subjects such as nuclear energy. The relationship a presenter has with their material can help with this. When a speaker really likes how they are conveying their message and what they are using to support the message, the presentation can come alive. Introducing interesting stories, perspectives and graphics can make all the difference.

I have noticed that speakers who come across as emotionally 'open' have a deeper connection to their audience. These speakers have a bit of vulnerability about them. I understand that not everyone is comfortable with this and I am not talking about exhibiting high levels of vulnerability. But allowing some vulnerability can help with coming across as natural or authentic. Research professor Brené Brown does a great job of explaining how vulnerability can be empowering. Have a look at her TED Talk: www.ted.com/talks/brene_brown_on_vulnerability

For some, a conference presentation is the last place they want to be vulnerable – even a tiny bit. Bear in mind that a lack of vulnerability can often feel like there is emotional armour plating around a speaker: no emotions are allowed out and audiences generally struggle to connect to these speakers.

Another way to connect to an audience is in the preparation stage. When starting to prepare a presentation, think about the emotional objective(s). Be clear about how you want the audience to feel when you have finished speaking. Do you want them to feel reassured? Excited? Concerned? Inspired? Involved? Use the emotional objective to guide how you interact with the audience; how you organise your ideas; the language you use; how you support ideas. All of these things will help increase audience connection. For more on the emotional objective as part of the BRIBE model see page 10.

A final thought on the power of emotion for influencing an audience: logic convinces but emotion commits.

Words to help connection

Another preparation tool to make content audience-focused and highly relevant is WIIFM: an acronym for What's In It For Me. The 'me' is the audience. I encourage you to be really clear in your mind about what your presentation can do for your audience. How can the audience use the information? How does it help them in their work life? Clarity on this and expressing it early on will help an audience connect to the content. If the presentation has high relevance, it gives the audience a powerful reason to listen closely.

How early do you need to say the WIIFM? Certainly within the first three or four minutes of a twenty-minute presentation. Again, for more discussion of WIIFM see page 14.

Stories to help connection

Using stories in a business presentation creates audience connection by generating significant activity in their brains. An effective story can engage up to seven regions of the brain. Different regions of the brain are triggered by specific descriptions in a story. This is why the advice on storytelling is to use sensory-rich language. Stories can activate areas of the brain responsible for:

1. Touch

2. Language processing

3. Language comprehension

4. Smell

5. Sounds

6. Movement

7. Colours/shapes.

As we know, to tell a story, the classic structure is three parts: beginning, middle and end. Begin with scene setting using multi-sensory language. Use the middle section to describe something significant that happens. The end is the place for a conclusion or insights.

A good case study of storytelling in practice is a presentation by Yves Morieux at consulting group, BCG. He is speaking about the productivity crisis in corporations and the story he tells is about a World Championship relay race.

Beginning	He sets the scene at the World Championships, describing the United States women's relay team as the clear favourites because they have two world champion runners in their team
Middle	The race taking place with an upset: the French team unexpectedly win gold
End	The insight that effective co-operation enabled the slower French team to beat the United States

Figure 14: Productivity story

Morieux then continues with the rest of his presentation, arguing that co-operation is the solution to improving productivity. See the full presentation at the following link: www.ted.com/talks/yves_morieux_how_too_many_rules_at_work_keep_you_from_getting_things_done#t-427272

The topic of storytelling is explained on page 42.

Use the body to help connection

Using our bodies to connect to a live audience is something that has been done for hundreds of years in the theatre. The big difference in business conferences is that a speaker will look directly at the audience. In the theatre it's more usual for the actors to look on stage and not directly at the audience.

I call where a speaker is looking the eyeline of the speaker or line of sight. Considering eye contact is such a quick and powerful way to connect with an audience, it's surprising how often I have to remind executives to look at the people they are speaking to.

There may be a number of reasons for their reluctance. Sometimes the issue is about confidence; sometimes it's about cultural practices. But it's important to overcome this reluctance if possible.

Eye contact is most effective when it combines scanning and holding. Scanning is looking across the whole audience: from left to right and from the front to the back of the room. I often record the presentations of people I am teaching. They can be quite surprised to see on the recordings that they have completely ignored one side of the room by giving them no eyeline.

Scanning the audience regularly enables you to see what's going on for the audience. Are they listening? Are they restless? Are they interested? What feedback are you getting and do you need to respond?

Holding eyeline is when you express a single thought to one person and hold eye contact with them while you do it. This is really good for improving the pace at which you speak. When you hold eye contact, you often settle at a speaking pace which is just right for the audience to follow you.

Another factor to consider regarding eye contact is speaker prompts. If you're using autocue your eyeline will already be directed towards the audience. You still need to actually look at the audience during pauses.

If you're reading a script it's wise to rehearse thoroughly so you can look up regularly at the audience and give them eye contact. For more information on using scripts effectively, see page 61.

Bullet points and mind maps are popular speaker prompts because they allow you to keep track of your ideas, sound fluent *and* maintain eyeline with an audience. Again, you do need rehearsal to give an audience maximum eyeline. There are more comments on eye contact on page 61.

Another quick fix for connecting to an audience is a simple smile. When speakers are uncomfortable or so focused on delivery and content, they can forget to smile. In truth, there are very few times when a smile is inappropriate. A soft smile or a bright smile can transform how your audience interacts with you. It animates your face and eyes and also has a positive effect on the quality of your voice. So smile!

Presentation needs more impact

How can I increase my impact? I get this question a lot. My advice is pay attention to crafting the message and look at your stage presence. My points below about developing the message are taken from the BRIBE model that's fully discussed in the first five chapters of this book. Go to page 9. The two elements of BRIBE I will mention here are Begin Powerfully and Be Bold because they can deliver quick results for increasing the impact of what you are saying.

Begin powerfully for impact

The first few minutes of an executive presentation provide several opportunities for beginning powerfully. Using a Hook is particularly valuable. The Hook is the device a speaker uses to 'hook' the audience into a presentation; to get audience attention.

Examples of an effective Hook include an engaging short story – provided it also connects to or establishes the theme of the presentation. A lot of business presentations use striking or significant data at the beginning. The data is often presented on a slide – the more interesting or attractive the slide the better (see page 174 later in this chapter for tips on slides or page 48 for a discussion of graphics).

Quotes are also popular Hooks. They can bring qualities of profundity, pathos, humour, irony, drama, curiosity etc. depending on who you are quoting, what they are saying and the context in which it is taking place. There are plenty of websites providing quotes. One that caught my eye is BrainyQuote.com, where I came across two great quotes from American lawyer James C. Humes.

Every time you have to speak you are auditioning for leadership.

The art of communication is the language of leadership.[76]

When quoting a quote it is worth making sure your delivery skills help the audience to hear it. Take your time. Say the quote with emphasis. Include a Power Pause (much longer pause) before and after the quote. Maybe say the quote twice. Yves Morieux at BCG provides a good example of how to deliver a quote in his presentation about the productivity crisis in corporations.

At the top of the presentation Yves Morieux quotes Paul Krugman, a Nobel Prize winner in economics and a New York Times columnist. Quoting Paul Krugman immediately brings a credibility and authority to the presentation.

The quote is:

Productivity is not everything, but in the long run, it is almost everything.[77]

Morieux delivers the quote at a good pace for comprehension. He emphasises the word 'almost'. He pauses immediately after the quote, giving the audience time to register the quote. The quote sets up the discussion that follows. Morieux goes on to explain that productivity is everything because it drives the prosperity of society and if productivity is in peril, it is a big problem requiring an urgent solution.

If quotes or data don't quite fit the presentation you have in mind, consider other elements of a powerful beginning: a story as discussed earlier in this chapter and elsewhere or pictures. A strong image can go a long way in getting attention and focusing on a core theme.

Be bold for impact

Be bold as you craft your message. By this I mean step outside the dull conventions of so many business presentations.

Take quotes for an example. I discussed using quotes above and illustrated an effective quote. However, there's a tendency in business presentations to use quotes that are a bit worthy, predictable or even dull. If we are bold, a quote might come from a person far removed from corporate life: a comedian, a movie character or even a rap star. If the person being quoted is surprising the quote will be more memorable. Remember, a surprising quote still needs to be tightly integrated into the theme or message of the presentation.

Other examples of being bold? I like the idea of departing occasionally from the typical tripartite structure of introduction, key points and conclusion.

A good example of this is a graduation speech given by England football manager, Gareth Southgate, at my daughter's school in 2017. The speech had two parts. The first part highlighted his best achievements in football (obviously highly impressive). At the start of the second part he explained that glorious achievements were not the whole story. He went on to describe disappointments, setbacks and lows he experienced in his career. As he described them he shared what he'd learned. He clearly learned a lot more from mistakes than from successes. His message to graduating schoolgirls about the importance of resilience was well made.

This example of a simple binary structure worked well and it could be adapted easily for business use. Indeed, I used it recently at a business networking event for the University of Sussex.

You can be bold with structure and you can be bold with language. Often the language of presentations is unnecessarily neutral. If our purpose is to give clear and compelling communication, then let's venture beyond management speak and low-impact language. Enriched language is passionate, has stories, poetry, quotes, metaphors and similes: used judiciously in a presentation these devices can clarify meaning in a compelling way.

I have a terrific example of a simile (when we say different things are like each other). In 2018, Brexit consumed the national conversation in the United Kingdom. A critic of Brexit and former top civil servant, Sir Martin Donnelly, described giving up the European customs union for free trade deals as like 'giving up a three-course meal now in favour of the promise of a packet of crisps'.

Similes like the one above make a point efficiently, clearly and with great impact.

One more thing to try if you want to be bold: music. Music features regularly at the start and end of conferences. There are times when it could also be used to start a conference speech. This often works better if the music is captivating *and* integral to the main message.

An example I am thinking of is an executive who played the well-known song 'Getting to Know You' from the musical *The King and I* by Rogers and Hammerstein. The song faded as she started speaking to an audience of 500 salespeople for the first time as their new head of division. The song charmingly emphasised the purpose of the presentation: to start building the new relationship between boss and colleagues in order to work well together.

I just have to share with you a really bold example of using music in a keynote speech. Midway through a speech to 250 executive coaches, the speaker suggested taking a short break.[78] She invited the audience to get on their feet to dance to 'I Feel Good' by James Brown. Amazingly, everybody did and there was an exuberant sense of joy in the room for a few precious minutes. Then it was back to a serious presentation discussing the difference between endurance and resilience.

Was the music integral to the business message? Maybe. The speaker was making the point that resilience requires recovery time. You could argue that the dance was a 'recovery' from the serious messages of the presentation. Or you could say it related to the closing comment 'Wake up. Don't squander your life': making the most of life means making time for joy as well as other things.

You could dismiss both arguments above and say the music was just about having fun unexpectedly. In any case the music worked in this context. Admittedly, this was in the ever-cool city of Santa Barbara in California. I am still asking myself whether I am brave enough to try this when I am speaking. Mmmm.

Presenter needs more stage presence

Crafting the message will get you so far in terms of improved impact. Investing in stage presence will help with the rest. Stage presence is about freeing the voice and body to express a business message powerfully and using executive style to provide positive presence.

Voice work for stage presence

Getting vocally ready for a presentation is like doing a sound check before a show. The purpose is to achieve the best possible sound to convey ideas to an audience.

The foundation of voice is breath and the foundation of a good voice is diaphragm breathing. The diaphragm is a muscle that expands downwards to allow air in and contracts upwards to push air up and out of the body. The more effectively you use the diaphragm, the more breath you will have to power the voice.

Try this simple exercise to make sure you have the mechanics of diaphragm breathing right.[79]

1. Put your hands flat on your tummy – roughly in line with the navel. Have the middle finger of one hand in the navel.

2. Make a vigorous 'Sh' sound. Then a longer 'Shhhhhh-hhhh' sound moving your navel inwards. You should feel this action with your finger and hands.

3. When there's no more air, let your navel move outwards to bring in more air. As you do this the diaphragm moves downwards to allow a big intake of air.

See page 74 for more information on diaphragm breathing.

The voice can sound even better when you keep an upright posture with shoulders down and chest open. This makes it easier for air to travel out of the body.

Tension in the body affects the voice negatively so be aware of where you typically feel tension. The usual spots are shoulders, neck, temples and jaw. Spend time relaxing the areas of tension. I like rotating my shoulders forwards and backwards and often massage my neck, temples and jaw.

To give your message maximum vocal impact, consider the following:

Pace	Speaking too fast or slow. Most people tend to be a little too fast.	Maintain a pace your audience can easily follow.
Pause	Not pausing between, and at the end of, sentences. Not pausing between key points.	Effective pausing aids comprehension. Use a Power Pause between key points in a presentation and after a critical point. Power Pauses last significantly longer than regular pauses.
Articulation	Poor articulation undermines the clarity of a message. Poor articulation is a real challenge in international meetings where English is a second language for members of the audience.	The solution is so easy. It requires the speaker to make quite a lot more effort when forming words. Open the mouth more; work the lips and tongue more. Practise tongue twisters before a presentation to prime the articulators (mouth, lips, tongue).
Colour	A voice with little colour lacks energy, has a narrow range and doesn't contain enough emphasis.	To sound more energetic, breathe from the diaphragm. It helps to move the body to get oxygen flowing so (if possible) go for a short, brisk walk or run on the spot before speaking.

Figure 15: Vocal impact solutions

A voice with a narrow range is often described as monotone. Without fail, monotone voices have a negative impact on audiences.

Extending vocal range often means creating new speaking habits. Start to notice when your range is narrow. Is it all the time or in certain situations? Is there a trigger?

Alongside the self-awareness practice above do voice work. Try the following.

1. Get something to read aloud, e.g. poem, scripts or news copy. Get familiar with the content.

2. Get a phone or tablet and record yourself doing the following activities.

3. Read the words out loud in a normal voice.

4. Read the same words out loud in a slightly exaggerated voice.

5. Read the same words out loud in a highly exaggerated voice – much louder, more passionately, more energetically than you would ever do in real life.

6. Read the words again in a voice that is somewhere in the middle of normal and highly exaggerated.

7. Listen to the recordings. What do you notice?

Signature Style for stage presence

Another way to increase stage presence is with appearance. Dressing according to your Signature Style ensures you know how to make a positive impression. Knowing your Signature Style means knowing:

- The ideal presence you want to have in business situations
- Your style principles and qualities
- What colours suit your personal colouring
- What clothes suit your body shape.

For a detailed explanation of how to create and apply your Signature Style, see page 99.

Online presence is underwhelming

Online presentations can have a long shelf life. They're often recorded for others to download so it's worth doing the best job you can. Where do people go wrong? Stilted speech, talking too quickly, mumbling, poor posture, not expressing themselves clearly, low-level energy, unprofessional appearance, poor physical background, poor lighting.

There's lot of relevant advice in the points above on improving stage presence. In particular, take a look at the comments on making the most of your voice.

Online, your appearance is the first thing people will notice and especially the colours you are wearing. So choose colours that work best for you and work with your surroundings. If you want to find out which colours suit you, go to page 99 for the chapter on Signature Style.

Wearing light, dark, bright or soft colours have different effects on those watching you. High-contrast colours like black and white or navy and ivory will give a more authoritative, sharper look. Lighter shades and pastels will generally make you come across as more open and approachable. The subtleness of pastels don't always translate well online. The colour can wash out and just look white-ish. Bright colours bring a sense of energy and draw attention.

Colour creates part of your online impact and so does the style of clothes. Choose clothes that communicate your values and that of your organisation. Consider doing a Presence Audit (the three words that describe your ideal presence – more information on page 70). Grooming is essential online because the camera can be very unforgiving. Make sure your grooming is immaculate.

I encourage women to wear make-up for online presentations. A well-made-up face often provides a helpful shortcut to looking more professional, competent and likeable. Studies also indicate that moderate make-up helps women come across as trustworthy.[80]

Before you've said a word, your body language has been noticed and judged. Start with an open, upright posture with shoulders down and back. If possible do online presentations standing up as it will improve posture and allow you to speak expressively with your hands. Be aware of reducing tension in your jaw, throat, shoulders or stomach. Your voice will also sound more energetic if you stand and speak.

I would recommend composing a medium close-up shot (MCU). That means your body is visible from the chest upwards. The closeness of the image will help the audience see your eyes and connect more quickly to you. Facial expressions will be visible so be animated and smile when appropriate. Pay attention to the energy in your voice. Online meetings are static in nature. It's usually one camera and one shot (MCU as mentioned) so things can feel flat. Vocal energy, pace and good voice skills are transforming.

Pay attention to articulation. It aids understanding and increases impact. Too many people are lazy when speaking and don't make the best use of their jaw, lips and tongue to give clear, dynamic speech. Tongue twisters wake up your articulators ahead of an online presentation. For tongue twisters and more voice information, go to page 79.

Sound quality is not always great in online meetings with poor-quality microphones or speakers so it's vital to start speaking with a passionate and authoritative voice from the very first word. Diaphragm breathing will certainly help with this. Information on this technique is in this chapter on page 168 and also the chapter called 'Vocal presence' on page 69.

Online presentations are rather like TV presentations. They work better when the speaker keeps sentences short and clear. Try explaining one idea per sentence. Online audiences find this communication style more engaging. A more conversational tone suits this medium but not to the extent of sounding too chatty.

When I presented a new show on TV we would always do a 'dry run'. That's a very detailed rehearsal of everything in real time and real conditions: scripts, lights, cameras, studio set, full make-up and clothes. It's the best way to get a complicated show absolutely right. Online presentations don't usually need that level of detail but important ones do benefit from rehearsals. Rehearse as if it were the real thing, so in the actual room if possible with the same lighting conditions and wearing work clothes.

Rehearsals are a good time to try out notes or prompts to see how effective they are. It might help to pin notes to the left or right of the camera so you can maintain train of thought and direct eye contact. Looking directly at the audience helps establish trust.

Bullet points usually work better than full scripts as you will sound more natural and maintain crucial eyeline with the camera. Also think about using mind maps. For more information see page 37.

Record your rehearsals and forensically review and critique them. Assess your presence: voice, body language and appearance. Check how clearly and effectively you're expressing your ideas. Observe what's visible in the background of the shot and if the colours of your clothes are making the impact you want. Rehearse until you look and feel confident.

Presentation slides are not inspiring

Effective communication is clear and compelling. This applies equally to the speaker and the slides they use. All too often, slides succumb to the following pitfalls:

- Underwhelming
- Too much information
- Too many slides
- Poor visual discipline
- The presenter frequently has their back to the audience while looking at slides
- The speaker fumbles with the remote control.

Obviously, do avoid all the above.

In addition, consider the relationship you have with slides. How you interact with your slides will determine some of their success. Ask yourself: do you really like (or love) the slides in terms of how they look and the message they convey? Good slides, well used, will attract the attention of the audience and help maintain that attention. Great slides will *wow* the audience with their impact and you will be more excited when you use them.

There are a number of things you can do to improve slides. See page 48 for a longer discussion of graphics. Here I want to focus on using live graphics in a presentation. This is something I've recently been doing when teaching at INSEAD and also delivering webinars.

Working live with graphics in a presentation can bring a dynamic energy. It reminds me of the difference between presenting live television and recorded programmes. It's always more exciting to be live on air. Sometimes I've done recorded television programmes 'as live', which means we recorded the show as if it were a live event. It's a bit closer to the feel of live television but only a bit.

If using PowerPoint for live graphics, click on the pen or highlighter feature in slideshow mode. To focus audience attention on specific data I use the pen to circle or underline a word or mark with a coloured highlighter.

More exciting is doing simple sketches as I did in a webinar explaining the different resonating chambers in the human body. I wanted to highlight the importance of the throat in resonance because it contains the voice box or vocal folds. When speaking I described the vocal folds as the crown jewels of the voice and sketched a basic crown shape. See the before and after in Figure 16.

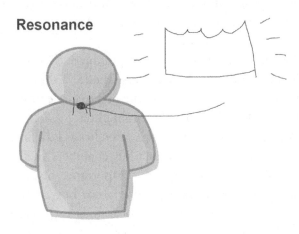

Figure 16: Live graphics example

I will confess that fear of drawing is something that held me back initially. I told myself I couldn't draw and this wasn't for me. But I got over that pretty quickly when I understood how business messages are transformed with live drawing and writing. It was also clear that you don't need to be at all skilled to use this technique.

I got a lot of help and encouragement from my friend and colleague Dr Penny Pullan, specialist in project management using graphics. She says: 'When that annoying parrot on your shoulder appears – the one that says you just can't draw and that you shouldn't even try – find a soundproof enclosure for it, lock it away and then start drawing!'[81]

I also recommend a very old book called *Graphics for Presenters: Getting Your Ideas Across* by Lynn Kearny, Crisp Publications, 1996. It's just so good. It is long since out of print but it's still possible to get used copies.

Summary

This chapter covered strategies for common pitfalls. They are:

To connect to an audience:

- Use emotion
- Make messages highly relevant to an audience
- Use stories
- Use eye contact

To increase impact:

- Use a Hook at the beginning
- Be bold

To increase stage presence:

- Breathe into the diaphragm
- Extend vocal range
- Develop a Signature Style
- Maintain a positive posture

To improve online presence:

- Choose clothes carefully
- Women, wear make-up
- Have immaculate grooming
- Articulate well and speak with energy to compensate for poor microphones
- Do a 'dry run' for important presentations

To improve slides:

- Use live graphics

Reflective questions

- Are you a passionate speaker?
- Do you come across as authentic? If not, why?
- What's the WIIFM (What's In It For Me) of your presentation?
- What story would make your Beginning powerful?
- What story embodies the theme of your presentation?
- How do you feel about storytelling? Why?
- What Hook have you chosen?
- Is the structure of your presentation bold?
- Are you using bold quotes?
- What's your vocal challenge? Pace, pause, articulation or colour?
- What aspects of your Signature Style do you want to use in your presentations?
- How positive is your posture?
- Are your slides inspiring? What needs to change?
- Will you do a dry run?

Chapter 14

MANAGE NERVES

'How do I manage nerves?' is the mother of all presentation questions. More people ask this than anything else. Originally this chapter did not exist. I wrote a short tip on nerves in the next chapter on top tips but I wasn't entirely happy with it. I had a feeling I wasn't doing the topic justice, bearing in mind how important it is for so many people.

Then I thought back to the approach of my first book, *Voices of Experience*, where I sought opinions, views and insights on presentations from many different people. And suddenly I had a model for this chapter: it is voices of experience on the topic of nerves. In addition to my own tips on nerves, I have ideas from a number of top professionals. I am so grateful to them for sharing their experiences so generously. I love this chapter for its unique insights and suggestions.

My view on nerves is they often occur when a speaker is under-prepared or 'winging it'. Time is often a challenge in our busy business lives yet successful leaders always invest time in preparing presentations.

Nerves can be a good indication of being in a focused and alert state ahead of a presentation. The problem starts when nerves overwhelm a speaker and get in the way of communication.

When this happens pay attention to breathing. If it becomes rapid and shallow, bring it under control. Slow down and breathe deeply. Pay attention to tense areas of your body and try to release some of the tension. Spend a minute or so beforehand doing a mental rehearsal (see page 151). See yourself getting your message across successfully. Hold that feeling as you prepare to speak.

Preview

- Preparation, preparation, preparation!
- Tell stories
- Four strategies for nerves
- Interact
- Focus
- Anti-nerve technique
- Outside in – Use image

Preparation, preparation, preparation!

If you are prepared the nerves are manageable.

It is the easiest advice to give but it is the most difficult to do in practice because of the time factor.

I keep my diary free the hour before a presentation to do last minute adjustments. It's important not to rush into a presentation: not to go from one meeting straight into a presentation.

I also schedule two hours for preparation two days before. That time is protected to allow me to get prepared.

The time you spend on a business presentation beforehand makes a lot of difference in terms of nuance. It helps get the right words especially if content is more personal.

I did a TED-style talk recently. I started work on it three to four weeks beforehand.

The preparation for that included keeping sentences short and taking a break after each sentence. I tried a new technique of silently inserting a word in-between sentences – I chose "Hallelujah"! It made every sentence feel important and it really worked for me.

I was speaking to an audience of three hundred people so I also practiced delivering each sentence personally to a single person and the next sentence to a different person. It helped to focus on the text and the audience.

My overall process of preparation is to focus on the storyline, fine tune then cut off. None of this is done the day before.

One way to get rid of nerves is to share what you're feeling with the audience. I saw a colleague doing his first ever presentation. He was stumbling quite a bit. Then suddenly he told the audience it was the first time he'd ever spoken in front of an audience. After saying that he was completely at ease.

Rutger Schellens

CEO

ABN AMRO Clearing Bank

* *

Tell stories

Focus on storytelling if you are nervous about doing a presentation.

A lot of organisations are more comfortable with Excel than Word but there's a limit to what numbers will do. They will take you so far with the rational brain but you have to tell stories to connect at an emotional level. You want the audience to relate to you.

Look for stories you can tell which create a bond with the audience and for which they can see the relevance. Take the audience on a journey with you through your presentation so when you get to the call to action the audience think 'I like this person, I've listened to what they have to say and now they've asked me to do something – why wouldn't I do that?'

If you were doing the presentation to your mother or a child think about what stories bring to life what you're trying to say?

For example, I was leading a pitch to a major pharmaceutical group. It was the largest pitch I'd ever done – worth over one million euros a year. At the end of the meeting we were told we'd been selected to go forward to the final pitch.

When they mentioned the date I knew it was the day I'd arranged to take my eighty-year-old father to Mount Athos in Greece. I said to the people present "I need to tell you a story".

In August 1944 there was a young second lieutenant who was told he had to take three boats from Thessaloniki to Mount Athos to liberate 10th-century monasteries which were being harassed by Communist guerrillas. That second lieutenant was my father and I am taking him back to Mount Athos on the same day as the final pitch.

They loved it! It said something about the values of the organisation that they felt work was important but people were also important. The meeting went ahead without me and we won the pitch!

Telling stories can be a very effective way of presenting information. Each story has got a moral, a new take away and a structure and it creates connection.

For some people nerves show up as an obsession with content. Even during rehearsal these people spend all their time re-writing the speech.

The truth is unless the content is really bad nobody will remember what's said. What people will come away with is an impression. This is formed from a series of questions. Is this speaker somebody I want to invest my time in? Is this someone I want to follow? Is this someone who's going to inspire me?

Nerves can make people spend a lot of time on content but then they go off piste straight out of the gate. I remember one executive who did this and he never went back on piste and his credibility was damaged. Watching his presentation was the longest seventeen minutes of my life.

Some people are naturally good at communication. If you're looking at yourself and your skills and think that public speaking is a weakness, it is something you can learn. There are techniques to help the message and body language, positioning, voice, cadence and timing. And technology like autocue can also help. It is interesting how some people think they don't need coaching but they really do.

And some people don't listen and become their own worst enemy. Not listening to feedback can damage the reputation of leaders.

So I get paid to tell stories and I enjoy telling stories. When I'm doing public speaking I tend to use a series of stories to illustrate ideas and create an emotional bond. When the numbers get dropped in to prove a point the audience are in a better frame of mind to accept it.

I actually enjoy public speaking. I still remember at the age of six I was taken to a pantomime and when actors asked people to come up on stage I leapt up. I remember singing "I'm a cow called Daisy" and conducting the audience with a Smarties packet attached to my finger. My future was mapped out right there.

Paul Abrahams

Head of Corporate Communications

RELX GROUP

* *

Four strategies for nerves

The first point is authenticity. Being comfortable in your own skin helps effective communication yet so many people try to wear another skin.

It's also about being comfortable in your own language. Often people feel compelled to use management speak or business speak instead of plain speaking.

For many people public speaking is a daunting experience. I am not a natural. For years I was terrified of speaking in public and turned down being a prefect at school and being best man at a wedding. Then at the age of thirty one I confronted the fear and made a career out of public speaking.

When I am teaching groups and we come to the topic of nerves, people find it reassuring to know everyone *in the group has a level of anxiety. My view is that even people who seem 'natural' at public speaking are just better at hiding nerves.*

Nerves come from adrenalin and you need a certain amount to perform so it's a matter of managing them. The time to feel nervous is when you don't feel nerves.

My nerves start 10-15 minutes before I speak. I get butterflies. Within two minutes those butterflies are in formation.

To synchronize the butterflies it helps to be self aware. Understand how your nerves are displayed. Often it's inside your body and not obvious to other people.

If your nerves are transmitting externally have a coping strategy. I know I will get dry mouth two times in a year so I have water everywhere: at the lectern, stage right and stage left.

Nerves also come from our inner voice. It can be our biggest critic or best advocate. Lord Coe told me that athletes at the start line of a race always have an inner voice. What's in your head and what the voice says will determine whether you win or lose.

Another thing athletes do is to change their view of nerves: to see them as fuel to perform. There's a great quote from Dave Alred, Jonny Wilkinson's kicking coach. He says,

'Feeling nervous? Maybe uncomfortable? Great! *It's your fuel for a great performance.'*

When I am training leaders I ask them to bring draft scripts of their presentation. The first thing I ask them to do is to change all commas and semi-colons into full stops. That immediately creates short sentences that are easier to deliver well and it makes speakers pause.

So to handle nerves:
- *Acknowledge everyone gets nervous*
- *Manage the butterflies*
- *Have a positive inner voice*
- *Change your view of nerves*

Jeff Grout

Motivational Business Speaker, Author and expert on People and Performance

* *

Interact

This tip is one I have used for myself and shared with executive clients.

Start with something interactive. This happens before you say the opening sentence of the actual presentation. It could be a comment or a question to do with getting to the presentation or about what it's like being there.

The goal is to get the audience doing something: either saying something back to you, raising their hands or nodding their heads. The audience could be reacting to a question about who is very familiar with the topic or who has strong views on the topic. The speaker could be addressing busy executives, acknowledging the strain attending a presentation generates for them as they are forced to leave their desks when they are under so much pressure.

Speak in a conversational tone to the audience and get them to interact before the presentation actually starts. This helps develop connection to the audience. It also means you've heard your voice so you feel less nervous. It breaks the silence and expectation that can weigh heavy at the start of a presentation and it helps the speaker feel grounded.

Brenda Ross

Executive Coach specialising in Leaders in Transition
Brenda Ross Associates

* *

Focus

Focus on what you can control in a presentation. You can control what you know, your arguments, how much you care about the subject and your outcome.

Panic breathing. When nervous our breathing speeds up and we get a running breath. This is when you need to focus on sentence structure. Put a mental full stop and breath between sentences. This will give your body an opportunity to breathe.

If you are in a private space take in a breath through the nose and let go of the muscles in the tummy area or shoulders. Breathe out through the mouth. Focus on the out breath. Breathe out longer and slower than the in breath.

If people can see you seated around a table or on a panel try this quick fix. Breathe in through the nose and on the slow out breath make a silent 'ff' sound. Do this several times to restore control.

Remember that breathing alone cannot rescue a presentation that lacks clarity, preparation and rehearsal.

Michaela Kennen

Voice and Dialect Coach

(see page 84 for more advice from Michaela on developing the voice)

* *

Anti-nerve technique

For most, fear of public speaking is a vague fear of the unknown: a fear that something dreadful will happen during the speech. It is often very difficult to pin down exactly what it is you are scared of.

The key to conquering nerves is to change your vague, negative thoughts into specific positive thoughts.

In the last few hours before the speech, keep thinking about all the work you have done to prepare a brilliant script. Allow yourself to be proud of it.

And then, in the last 5 minutes before you are on, focus on just one thing: the first line of your script. Keep repeating the line in your mind.

And if you keep your thoughts focused relentlessly on your first words, your mind does not have the energy to feel nervous as well.

Graham Davies

Presentation Coach

* *

Outside in: Use image

You build confidence from the inside out, but you can also help to build it from the outside in.

If you look the part it helps you feel confident because people respond to you the way you want. Use your image to trigger how you expect to be treated.

When doing workshops I sometimes give a male participant a pair of slippers to wear. Eventually I ask how he felt dressed in business clothes and slippers. The reply is always that he felt disadvantaged the whole way through. What you wear will affect you internally as well as the message you give.

When you're groomed and appropriately dressed you get the response you want from people. It's the same idea as 'dress for the job you want not the job you have'.

When it comes to your image be the person that manages the signals you're giving; take control and don't leave it to chance. People will make judgements anyway so you might as well stack the odds in your favour and feel more confident doing it.

Jennifer Aston

Image Coach

Chapter 15

TOP TEN TIPS

IN THIS FINAL chapter I share my top ten tips for presentation mastery.

- Pay attention to recovery
- Make the most of Q&A
- Face the discomfort of difficult messages
- Do your best with last-minute presentations
- How to present in a second language
- Keep to time
- Go naked!
- Be ambitious with team presentations
- Get feedback
- Be bold

No. 1 Pay attention to recovery

Recovering well from a mistake is the hallmark of a skilled business presenter.

It's just as true of television news anchors. I often watch TV anchors to see what happens when things go wrong. The pros barely skip a beat. They pause and move smoothly on. Those still learning their craft often make a big deal of a mistake and unfortunately the audience ends up remembering the mistake. The trick is to stay in control.

Deep diaphragm breathing will help with anxiety and enable you to regain control. Pausing will give valuable moments to regain composure and to order thoughts.

My advice is to go into a presentation expecting *something* unexpected to happen. It could be the autocue breaking down, it could be the microphone malfunctioning or even your speaker notes cascading to the floor. In any case the outcome is not to deliver a perfect presentation, as in this you will inevitably fail. The outcome is to deliver the best presentation you can in the circumstances. If you expect to make minor mistakes or find yourself in unexpected situations, this primes you for more effective recovery if things do go wrong.

No. 2 Make the most of Q&A

Q&A presents an excellent opportunity for speakers to develop the relevance of their message to an audience and to involve the audience. As you commence Q&A, good questions to ask yourself include: what else do the audience need to know from me? How can I help them even more? The Q&A is also a valuable moment to 'read' the audience to get a sense of how the message is being received. What is the body language of the audience telling you? Are they curious? Confused? Inspired?

To answer the above, invite questions from your audience and also ask *them* questions. At the preparation stage it is useful to anticipate likely questions. It might also be worth thinking about worst-case questions and how you want to approach them.

Message discipline in the Q&A helps it become a strong and integral part of a presentation. There are a number of things you can do to achieve this. As you answer questions, repeatedly link to the theme of the presentation. Refer back to specific points from the presentation to reinforce ideas. It's often useful to have a few new examples of the points you made so the Q&A feels fresh. You might want this information on a backup slide to be used if appropriate.

In addition to message discipline I encourage event discipline. Q&A is an event within an event. It's part of a presentation and at the same time distinct from the presentation. It's an important event for the audience so let them know early on when Q&A will happen – preferably in the introduction of the presentation. When you actually start the Q&A, explain the format and how much time is available.

It's a good practice to repeat a question to make sure everyone has heard it properly. This also gives the presenter time to think about how they will answer the question.

One way to manage questions is to ask for clarification questions first. This helps the audience focus their thoughts and makes asking the first question less onerous.

Stay in control when you get hostile questions – notice if you need to pause and breathe deeply. The temptation to dismiss a hostile question is sometimes a missed opportunity. Try to discern if the questioner is raising something useful for the wider audience. Don't lose your cool. A presentation will always be enhanced when the speaker is effective at managing hostile questions. The reverse is also true: poor handling of an antagonistic questioner diminishes the speaker.

Watch out for people hogging question time. It may well be a case of deep curiosity or high enthusiasm on the part of the questioner. The problem is that Q&A very quickly feels lopsided or unbalanced when it's dominated by one person. To remedy this, when I am introducing Q&A I often say I will take one question per person.

Do make the audience aware of when you are bringing Q&A to a close. Use the closing moments to recap the overall theme or message and leave the audience with a final thought: perhaps a call to action, a quote or memorable picture.

No. 3 Face the discomfort of difficult messages

From time to time executives will be required to present difficult messages. For example, it could be announcing redundancies or other painful organisational change. These events will never be easy but there are things you can do to make the best of the situation.

As you work out what to say and how you will say it, pay attention to how you are feeling. What level of discomfort are you feeling ahead of the presentation? What's driving the discomfort? Do you want to share your feelings with the audience? Is it appropriate to do so?

When you start speaking observe the evident feelings of the audience. Try to connect with where they're at in what you say and do.

In such situations your presence will be scrutinised. People will note whether you come across as authentic, caring, respectful and transparent.

A colleague gave me a remarkable example of how one CEO handled the announcement of 200 redundancies. He chose to give the difficult message face-to-face in the form of a presentation. He spent more time than usual thinking about what to say beforehand.

When he spoke to staff it was with sensitivity and awareness of their feelings. He was transparent about the difficult situation the company was in.

He spent a lot of time thanking staff. He expressed appreciation for their valuable contribution to the business, for their loyal service over many years, that each of them had given so much of themselves in their work for the company.

Staff obviously felt his words were genuine because at the end of the speech they got to their feet and *applauded* the

CEO. He obviously got many things right as that is rare in such a delicate situation.

No. 4 Do your best with last-minute presentations

Last-minute requests for a presentation can be quite nerve-racking.

They remind me of being in the newsroom when a big story breaks. Initially there's semi-panic then moments later professionalism and discipline kicks in. The editor makes the decision about what to do in the time available before the next bulletin. If there's virtually no time the editor might include a few lines of script about the story at the top of the bulletin. A bit more time and it's a paragraph of the news story with a still picture or a map. Any more time and it's a live interview with a reporter or eyewitness.

It's similar for an executive presenter doing a last-minute presentation. In the first instance the focus is on what can be done in the time available. Keep in mind the purpose of the presentation and what the audience specifically want or need from the speaker.

When doing last-minute presentations I find it useful to have a framework I can deploy any time anywhere. I limit myself to a maximum of three key points which form the middle of the presentation. If there's time I brainstorm to refine the key points and explain them with supporting points (limited to a maximum of three). Once key points and supporting points are clear, I think about how to illustrate the ideas: perhaps with data, a slide or stories.

I then focus on the start of the presentation and also how I will end it. If there's time for a rehearsal I do one. If not, I will spend a minute or two doing a mental rehearsal of the presentation (for more on mental rehearsals see page 150).

Moments before speaking I make sure I am breathing deeply using my diaphragm to help steady nerves. I typically maintain a cautious pace. A slightly slower, more controlled pace can give valuable thinking and processing time.

In the end you can only do your best.

No. 5 Presentations in a second language

Many executives I teach are required to do presentations in a language that is not their mother tongue. This can generate quite a bit of anxiety because it throws up a number of challenges.

It can be difficult to come across as naturally as you would when speaking in your primary language. It can also be tricky if you can't find a precise word at a given moment or if you lose your line of thought. There's often a frustrating feeling that speaking can never be as good as presentations in your mother tongue because you just don't have as many words to express ideas.

There's good advice from colleagues who've faced these challenges successfully. Start by accepting that the presentation might not be as good as mother-tongue presentations. But you can still do well if you prepare a lot more than you usually do. In addition to planning the content, plan the words you need and focus on vocabulary you don't know that will help.

One suggestion is to keep to simpler themes and words as it is easier for things to go wrong if attempting something highly ambitious.

It sometimes works to share a light-hearted comment about the language challenge you are facing with the audience. This can lighten things up for the speaker and audience. When a speaker is struggling with language and is anxious about it, audiences often feel uncomfortable. A light-hearted, humble comment considered in the planning stage can make quite a difference.

A senior Dutch executive I have worked with has another approach. Ahead of delivering a presentation in a second language (in his case English) he primes his language skills. When speaking in Dutch all day he can find himself searching for English words when presenting in his second language. His solution is to speak in English to himself (and others) during the day of the presentation.

No. 6 Keep to time

I've seen so many presentations run over time and I cannot understand why. It is relatively easy to keep to time and it gives such a professional impression. I know I come from a news background where things have tightly fixed time slots and it feels as if there's never enough time. Yet it's that very time-pressed environment of TV news that gives us a useful tool for timekeeping.

Television news uses a *Running Order* (sometimes called a rundown) to hold a show together and keep to strict time. It is basically a glorified agenda that lists all the items of a show. Beside each item is its duration and the live running time of the show. I have simplified and adapted a TV running order for executive presentations in Figure 17. The example is for a presentation that lasts 20 minutes with five minutes for Q&A. The presentation starts at 9.00am.

Running order

- 30-minute time slot
- 20-minute presentation + 5-minute Q&A
- Start time: 9.00 am
- End time: 9.25 am

Item	Detail	Support	Duration	Start time
1	Introduction	Title slide	3 minutes	9.00 am
2	Point 1	Slides	5 minutes	9.03 am
3	Point 2	Video	5 minutes	9.08 am
4	Point 3	Slides	5 minutes	9.13 am
5	Conclusion	Slide	2 minutes	9.18 am
6	Q&A	-	5 minutes	9.20 am
-	Finish	-		9.30 am
			Total duration 30 minutes	

Figure 17: Running order

A few things to bear in mind when using a running order. Always allow for a few minutes' slippage; so for a '30-minute' presentation practise speaking for 25 minutes. Late starts, technical delays, nerves, pausing etc. can all eat into presentation time so it's best to have some room for manoeuvre.

In Figure 17 I have illustrated a presentation and Q&A in a 30-minute time slot. The running time of the whole event is 25 minutes, which gives five minutes for slippage. If you do find yourself with the five minutes still available, it is easy to extend the Q&A and/or take the opportunity to pull together the main points in the presentation and Q&A.

Place a watch or a small clock in front of you so you can see time passing and how close you are to your ideal time. That way you can take your time if you're ahead and cut out things if you're behind.

Rehearsing is necessary to keep to time. A short presentation is easy enough to rehearse all the way through. If it's a long presentation, I recommend rehearsing individual sections of the presentation first to compare the time you've assigned versus the actual time it takes. Then move on to rehearsing the complete presentation with a stopwatch.

No. 7 Go naked!

When I am teaching I encourage executives to do naked presentations and this certainly gets everyone wide-eyed and sitting upright. I smile softly as I explain 'naked' presentations are when speakers communicate without the usual trappings of slides. In these presentations it is all about the speaker's presence powering the message and connecting deeply with an audience.

I call these *naked presentations* because many people feel a certain vulnerability when communicating in this mode. There's nowhere to hide and nothing to hide behind. It's just the speaker and the audience. There's a directness and simplicity to this form of spoken communication that can be immensely powerful for gaining trust and conveying a compelling vision.

It's my view that executives should have the versatility to speak in different modes including 'naked'. It is challenging to do this well and it requires the speaker to have strong presence.

The voice does a lot of the heavy lifting to capture and maintain audience attention. The voice also needs much greater clarity than for other presentation styles, and this is achieved through articulation, pace and pausing. The heightened vocal clarity sharpens audience understanding. The voice has another crucial role: to communicate passion and other emotional objectives (see page 69 for more on developing the voice).

Alongside vocal competence, the language of a naked presentation is important. Clarity is king and queen. Ideas have to be clearly expressed so that comprehension feels effortless for the audience. The impact will also come from using enriched language, that is, stories, similes, metaphors and word pictures.

Alliteration is worth considering because it can bring colour to language and even a sense of fun (if appropriate). Alliteration means saying a group of words that start with the same letter. Examples include 'lots of lively leaders' or 'excited execs'.

If you want a lighter tone in parts of a presentation you could combine alliteration with a form of poetry called a limerick. This is a highly rhythmic short poem that works well with alliteration. To illustrate, on the spur of the moment, I have created a limerick about myself below.

There once was a woman named Jacqui

Whose purpose was just to be happy

When she started to write

It tested her might

And so she became super snappy!

I am sure you can do much better than that. The point is that using enriched language in naked presentations serves up interesting possibilities for engagement.

No. 8 Be ambitious with team presentations

Team presentations can be terrifically dynamic and exciting but they do require thought and preparation to make the most of the format.

Think about the roles of different speakers in a team presentation. There are several configurations that work well.

- Two 'anchors' can introduce the presentation (double header in TV speak) and 'throw' to other speakers as well as end the presentation
- One 'anchor' can introduce the presentation, subsequent speakers and conclude the presentation
- Everyone can speak in turn covering a single point
- Speakers can deliver two points at a time
- One person is assigned to manage Q&A.

Some additional thoughts. If you are using slides, think about how you will operate the slides. Sometimes it works passing a remote control from one speaker to another – sometimes this looks a little awkward. Another option would be to assign the slides to a single member of the team or to a third party that is not part of the team of speakers.

It looks better if everyone 'on stage' has a clear role. It does seem odd if one or more people do not take part. If this is the case, it's worth explaining why to the audience.

If you want to bring slickness and polish to the team presentation, consider using a running order as explained on page 196. Mark up the running order so it's clear when each member of the team is speaking.

It almost goes without saying that you will need to rehearse a team presentation. If you record the rehearsal, pay attention to where team members are looking when a colleague is speaking and how they are looking. Remember you are still 'on stage' even when someone else is speaking. The audience will always see bored or nervous faces or awkward posture. If everyone on stage looks at the speaker it drives the audience attention onto the speaker.

Use links to connect one point in a presentation to another. Examples include:

- Thank you…
- Next I will speak about…
- I have been speaking about *x*, my colleague will now speak about *y*…
- My colleague has been speaking about *x* and I will now speak about *y*…
- Slides make good visual links.

What you wear as a team might need attention. If it's important to look like a team, you might consider wearing a common colour or adopting a similar style of clothes. Colour and style can give an audience a quick visual message that you are an established and strong team.

No. 9 Seek feedback

As you become a more accomplished speaker, it is easy to get into a rut: always doing the same thing the same way. To keep executive presentations dynamic and fresh, and to keep yourself challenged, seek continuous feedback. This gives you information to develop yourself and reveals blindspots. Consider getting a presentation buddy to regularly share and swap feedback. Review recordings of your work and assess yourself.

Get feedback from colleagues and participants attending your presentations. My Dutch colleague, Wim Dufourne, has a fantastic example of this: the After Action Review (AAR).

He suggests that after every meeting or presentation get feedback on the following:

- What worked well?
- What should I do differently next time?
- What should I celebrate?
- What do you think I didn't say?

The AAR should be short – only five minutes or so. The comments are not for debate but allow all participants to share their thoughts on the speaker's effectiveness.

Consider starting a presentation journal to regularly record feedback and your thoughts. Use it to track progress across a period of time or as you prepare a significant or particularly challenging presentation.

No. 10 Be bold!

Believe in yourself and be bold.

ENDNOTES

1   www.mayaangelou.com/blog

2   Aristotle, *The Art of Rhetoric*. Translated by H.C. Lawson-Tancred, Penguin Books, 2004, pp.16–17.

3   Paul Brown and Virginia Brown, *Neuropsychology for Coaches*, Open University Press, 2012, p.18.

4   'Why Your Brain Loves Good Storytelling', Paul J. Zak, *Harvard Business Review*, 2014.

5   Dan and Chip Heath, *Made to Stick*, Arrow Books, 2007, p.67.

6   Mark Forsyth, *The Elements of Eloquence – How to Turn the Perfect English Phrase*, Icon Books, 2013.

7   *The Mail on Sunday*, 3 June 2018.

8   Dan and Chip Heath, *Made to Stick*, Arrow Books, 2007.

9   Allan and Barbara Pease, *The Definitive Book of Body Language*, Orion, 2005, p.189.

10 Simon Sebag Montefiore, *Speeches That Changed The World*, Quercus, 2010, p.144.

11 *The Elements of Eloquence*, Mark Forsyth, Icon Books, 2013.

12 Allan and Barbara Pease, *The Definitive Book of Body Language*, Orion, 2005, p.357.

13 Barbara Minto, *The Pyramid Principle: Logic in Writing and Thinking*, Pearson Books, 2009, p.7.

14 A much fuller explanation of the pyramid structure is in Barbara Minto's excellent book, *The Pyramid Principle: Logic in Writing and Thinking*, Pearson Books, 2009. Barbara's book is focused on organising written ideas; however, it works superbly for presentations.

15 Barbara Minto, *The Pyramid Principle: Logic in Writing and Thinking*, Pearson Books, 2009, p.15.

16 Jenny Rogers, *Building A Coaching Practice*, 2nd edition, McGraw Hill Education, 2017, p.123.

17 If you want more ideas on storytelling there's a particularly good chapter on how to tell stories in presentations in the book *TED Talks: The Official TED Guide to Public Speaking*, Chris Anderson, Headline Publishing, 2016, p.63.

18 Allan and Barbara Pease, *The Definitive Book of Body Language*, Orion, 2005, p.190. Visual and verbal presentations have a retention rate of 50% compared to 10% for just words alone.

19 Meg Miller, 'Eye Tracking Is Turning Design into a Science', 2017. www.fastcodesign.com/90131416/eye-tracking-is-turning-design-into-a-science

20 '10 Tips on How to Make Slides That Communicate Your Idea', 2014. https://blog.ted.com/10-tips-for-better-slide-decks/

21 Kendra Cherry, 'What Is The Serial Position Effect?', January 2017. www.explorepsychology.com/serial-position-effect/

22 Phil McAleer, Alexander Todorov and Pascal Belin (2014) 'How Do You Say "Hello"? Personality Impressions from Brief Novel Voices'. *PLoS ONE* 9(3): e90779. doi:10.1371/journal.pone.0090779

23 This wonderful phrase and concept comes from *The Art of Possibility, Transforming Professional and Personal Life* by Rosamund Stone Zander and Benjamin Zander, Harvard Business Review Press, 2000.

24 The concept is from *My One Word: Change Your Life with Just One Word* by Mike Ashcraft and Rachel Olsen published by Zondervan, 2012.

25 Adrian Furnham and Evgeniya Petrova, *Body Language in Business – Decoding the Signals*, Palgrave Macmillan, 2010. There is an insightful discussion of the complexity of the transmission and receiving of signals from body language.

26 Adrian Furnham and Evgeniya Petrova, *Body Language in Business – Decoding the Signals*, Palgrave Macmillan, 2010, p.57.

27 Adrian Furnham and Evgeniya Petrova, *Body Language in Business – Decoding the Signals*, Palgrave Macmillan, 2010, p.57.

28 Allan and Barbara Pease, *The Definitive Book of Body Language*, Orion, 2005.

29 Allan and Barbara Pease, *The Definitive Book of Body Language*, Orion, 2005, p.137.

30 Adrian Furnham and Evgeniya Petrova, *Body Language in Business – Decoding the Signals*, Palgrave Macmillan, 2010, p.143.

31 Ron Gutman, TED Talk, *The Hidden Power of Smiling*, 2011.

32 Adrian Furnham and Evgeniya Petrova, *Body Language in Business – Decoding the Signals*, Palgrave Macmillan, 2010, p.30.

33 Sarah Stevenson, 'There's Magic in Your Smile', *Psychology Today*, 25 June 2012.

34 Ron Gutman, TED Talk, *The Hidden Power of Smiling*, 2011.

35 Adrian Furnham and Evgeniya Petrova, *Body Language in Business – Decoding the Signals*, Palgrave Macmillan, 2010, p.32.

36 Ron Gutman, TED Talk, *The Hidden Power of Smiling*, 2011

37 Christopher Bergland, 'The Neuroscience of Speaking with Your Hands', *Psychology Today*, 5 July 2013.

38 University of Alberta, 'Hand Gestures Linked to Better Speaking', *ScienceDaily*, 11 May 2005. www.sciencedaily.com/releases/2005/05/050511105253.htm

39 Dr Fiona McPherson, cognitive psychologist. www.mempowered.com/strategies/gesturing-improve-memory-language-thought

40 Adrian Furnham and Evgeniya Petrova, *Body Language in Business – Decoding the Signals*, Palgrave Macmillan, 2010.

41 Allan and Barbara Pease, *The Definitive Book of Body Language*, Orion, 2005.

42 University of Alberta, 'Hand Gestures Linked to Better Speaking', *ScienceDaily*, 11 May 2005. www.sciencedaily.com/releases/2005/05/050511105253.htm

43 For further reading, see Trinny Woodall and Susannah Constantine, *The Body Shape Bible*, Weidenfeld & Nicolson, 2007 or Susan Moses, *The Art of Dressing Curves: Best-kept Secrets of a Fashion Stylist*, Harper Design, 2016.

44 Tina Bicat, *The Handbook of Stage Costume*, The Crowood Press, 2006.

45 Adrian Furnham and Evgeniya Petrova, *Body Language in Business – Decoding the Signals*, Palgrave Macmillan, 2010, p.57.

46 Adrian Furnham and Evgeniya Petrova, *Body Language in Business – Decoding the Signals*, Palgrave Macmillan, 2010, p.57.

47 Adrian Furnham and Evgeniya Petrova, *Body Language in Business – Decoding the Signals*, Palgrave Macmillan, 2010, p.64.

48 Robert Emmons, 'Three Surprising Ways That Gratitude Works at Work', *Greater Good Magazine*, 11 October 2017.

49 Robert Emmons mentions Globoforce as an example of a company that provides expertise on gratitude programmes in his article 'Three Surprising Ways That Gratitude Works at Work', *Greater Good Magazine*, 11 October 2017.

50 Definition from Ilene Schaffer, 'Mindful Stepping'.

51 https://greatergood.berkeley.edu/. This is part of the university's Happiness Project that explores the root of happiness and compassion.

52 Research led by Prathik Kini, the University of Indiana, 2015.

53 Hudson Institute of Coaching, *Certification Manual*, 2015.

54 Amy Cuddy, *Presence – Bringing Your Boldest Self to Your Biggest Challenge*, Orion Books, 2016, p.268.

55 Research by Prathik Kini, Joel Wong, Sydney McInnis, Nicole Gabana and Joshua W. Brown, 'The Effects of Gratitude Expression on Neural Activity', *Neuroimage* 128: 1–10, 2016.

56 Robert Emmons, 'Three Surprising Ways That Gratitude Works at Work', *Greater Good Magazine*, October 2017.

57 Robert Emmons, 'Three Surprising Ways That Gratitude Works at Work', *Greater Good Magazine*, October 2017.

[58] Jeff Huffman PhD, 'Can Gratitude Help you Recover from a Heart Attack?', *Greater Good Magazine*, January 2018.

[59] Research by Prathik Kini, Joel Wong, Sydney McInnis, Nicole Gabana and Joshua W. Brown, 'The Effects of Gratitude Expression on Neural Activity', *Neuroimage* 128: 1–10, 2016.

[60] Prathik Kini, Joel Wong, Sydney McInnis, Nicole Gabana and Joshua W. Brown, 'The Effects of Gratitude Expression on Neural Activity', *NeuroImage* 128: 1–10, 2016.

[61] In his discussion of this, Robert Emmons refers to earlier research he was involved with in 2002.

[62] This concept comes from The Intentional Change Theory by Richard Boyatzis.

[63] From the *Daily Telegraph*, science section, 12 March 2016, www.telegraph.co.uk/science/2016/03/12/humans-have-shorter-attention-span-than-goldfish-thanks-to-smart/

[64] Author of 'Perceptual Integration – The Mechanics of Awakening'. Gary Sherman has fifteen free recordings relating to developing attention and self-awareness so if this topic engages you, there's plenty to explore. Mike Normant attributes much of his content on this topic to Gary Sherman.

[65] This idea was created by the late academic Chris Argyris and is widely known in the work of Peter Senge in *The Fifth Discipline: The Art and Practice of the Learning Organization*, Random House Business Books.

The concept of the Ladder of Inference can also be used in reverse: you start at the top of the ladder with the action based on belief and work down the ladder to explore your thinking and assumptions. It is a useful process to explain to audiences your perspective and and to make your thinking and reasoning visible. When used in this way it is often called the Ladder of Advocacy.

66 These questions are from *Crucial Conversations* by Kerry Patterson, Joseph Grenny, Ron McMillan and Al Switzler, McGraw Hill, 2012 – a great book primarily to help with challenging one-to-one conversations. There is a good chapter on understanding and challenging our personal stories (pp.103–130).

67 Ethan Kross, *Psychology Today*, June 2015.

68 Mike Normant, *Coach Yourself Up Progamme Guide*, 2016, p.37.

69 James Bauman, 'The Gold Medal Mind', *Psychology Today*. Originally published in May 2000 and reviewed/updated in June 2016.

70 *The New York Times*, 23 February 2014.

71 COL Vanessa M Meyer, *Military Medicine*, January 2018, SP USA.

72 This references a discussion of athletes in flow in James Bauman, 'The Gold Medal Mind', *Psychology Today*. Originally published in May 2000 and reviewed/updated in June 2016.

73 Dr. Scott Williams, Department of Management, Raj Soin College of Business, Wright State University, Dayton, Ohio, 'Head Games: The Use of Mental Rehearsal to Improve Performance', March 2004.

74 James Bauman, 'The Gold Medal Mind', *Psychology Today*. Originally published in May 2000 and reviewed/updated in June 2016.

75 COL Vanessa M. Meyer, 'Sport Psychology for the Soldier Athlete: A Paradigm Shift', *Military Medicine* 183(7–8), 2018. https://doi.org/10.1093/milmed/usx087

76 BrainyQuote.com. Xplore Inc, 2018. 27 February 2018. www.brainyquote.com/quotes/james_humes_154730

77 www.ted.com/talks/yves_morieux_how_too_many_
rules_at_work_keep_you_from_getting_things_done#t-
427272

78 The keynote speaker was Claire Genkai Breeze at the
Hudson Coaching Conference, Santa Barbara, 2017.
Her speech was called 'The Near Enemy of Resilience is
Endurance'.

79 The technique is from Jeremy Fisher and Gillyanne Kayes,
This is a Voice, Wellcome Collection, 2016.

80 Research study by Nancy Etcoff, Harvard Medical School,
2011.

81 For more information on the work of Dr Penny Pullan, see
www.makingprojectswork.co.uk/

INDEX

21 Day Gratitude Challenge, 134

Abrahams, Paul, Head of Corporate Communications, RELX Group, 181
Angelou, Maya, 10
Apfel, Iris, 102
Aristotle, Greek Philosopher, 11, 22
Aston, Jennifer, image coach, 187

Bicat, Tina, costume designer, 113
Brainyquote.com, source of quotes, 164
Brown, Brené, 'The Power of Vulnerability', 29, 46
Brown, James, 'I Feel Good', 167

Cuddy, Amy, social psychologist, reframing nerves, 130

Davies, Graham, presentation coach, 187
Douglas, Michael, Hollywood actor, 88
Dufourné, Wim, After Action Review (AAR), 200

Eastwood, Clint, 20
Ebbinghaus, Hermann, the serial position effect, 56
Emerson, Ralph Waldo, quote, 18
Emmons, Robert, University of California, Davis, 128, 131

'Getting to Know You', song from musical 'The King and I', 166
Gibbs, Andrea, storytelling TEDx talk, 43
Greater Good Science Center, 128
Grout, Jeff, motivational business speaker and author, 183

Hardcastle, Paul, British recording artist, 27
Hepburn, Audrey, 101
Hudson, Russ, *The Enneagram*, 20

Kemper, Dr Kathi, Ohio State University gratitude meditation download, 134
Kennen, Michaela, voice coach, 84, 186
King, Martin Luther, Junior, 27
Krugman, Paul, economist, 164

MacMillan, Ann, CBC broadcaster, 51
McLean, Pamela, the Hudson Institute, California, 144
mental rehearsal, 150
Miller, George, psychologist, *The Magical Number Seven, Plus or Minus Two*, 39
Minto, Barbara, *Pyramid Principle*, 39
Mitchell, Suzy, photographer, 122
Morieux, Yves, BCG, storytelling, 160

Normant, Mike, self coaching, 138, 149

Obama, Michelle, 101

Prayer of gratitude, Church of England, 133
Prescott, Lord, 20
Presence Audit, 70—74
Prince Harry, 61, 65
Pullan, Dr Penny, graphics, 176

Rogers, Jenny, coaching expert, 42
Rosling, Professor Hans, 'The Joy of Stats', 49
Ross, Brenda, executive coach, 185
Rowling, JK, quote, 17

Sandberg, Sheryl, COO, Facebook, 15, 101
Schellens, Rutger, CEO, ABN Amro Clearing Bank, 180
Sherman, Gary, developing attention, 141

Southgate, Gareth, England Football Manager, speech, 165
Snow, Peter, BBC broadcaster, 51
Swartz, Heidi, executive coach, 72

The Oakland Tribune, 26
tongue twisters, 79
trombinoscope, 118

Voices of Experience by Jacqui Harper, 179

West, Kanye, rapper, case study, 58
Williamson, Marianne, 'Our Deepest Fear', 13

Made in the USA
Monee, IL
16 January 2020

20409944R00125